# Teach Yourself To Play Classical Guitar

• • • • • • • • • • • • • • • • • • • • • • • • • • • • • • • • • • • • • • •

**NATHANIEL GUNOD**

**Everything you need to know to start playing classical guitar now!**

 **ONLINE ACCESS INCLUDED**

---

  To access audio, TNT 2 software, and video, visit: **alfred.com/redeem**

*Enter this unique code:*

0042697-33174857

### TNT 2 SYSTEM REQUIREMENTS

**Windows**
XP, Vista, 7, 8
QuickTime 7.6.7 or higher
1.8 GHz processor or faster
1.4 GB hard drive space
2 GB RAM minimum
Speakers or headphones
Internet access for updates

**Macintosh**
OS 10.4 and higher (Intel only)
QuickTime 7.6.7 or higher
1.4 GB hard drive space
2 GB RAM minimum
Speakers or headphones
Internet access for updates

 Alfred Music
P.O. Box 10003
Van Nuys, CA 91410-0003
alfred.com

*No part of this book shall be reproduced, arranged, adapted, recorded, publicly performed, stored in a retrieval system, or transmitted by any means without written permission from the publisher. In order to comply with copyright laws, please apply for such written permission and/or license by contacting the publisher at alfred.com/permissions.*

Copyright © MMXIV by Alfred Music
All rights reserved. Printed in USA.

ISBN-10: 1-4706-1506-1 (Book & Online Video/Audio/Software)
ISBN-13: 978-1-4706-1506-2 (Book & Online Video/Audio/Software)

Audio recording performed by Martha Masters.

Cover photo of antique guitar and interior photo of author: Tim Becker, Creative Image Photography, Manchester, CT.
Cover photo of Rodriquez guitar: courtesy of Fender Musical Instruments Corporation.

 **Alfred Cares.** Contents printed on environmentally responsible paper.

# CONTENTS

| | |
|---|---|
| **INTRODUCTION** | 3 |
| **PARTS OF THE GUITAR** | 4 |
| **THE CLASSICAL GUITARIST'S TOOL KIT** | 4 |
| **TUNING THE GUITAR** | 5 |
| **THE HANDS** | 6 |
|    Left-Handed Players | 6 |
| **FINGERNAILS** | 6 |
| **SEATING POSITION** | 7 |
| **THE GUITAR FINGERBOARD** | 8 |
|    ● Mini Guitar Lesson: Half Steps and Whole Steps | 8 |
| **READING MUSIC: PITCH** | 9 |
|    Notes | 9 |
|    The Staff | 9 |
|    Clefs | 9 |
| **READING MUSIC—TIME** | 10 |
|    Note Durations | 10 |
|    Rests | 10 |
|    Measures | 10 |
|    Time Signatures | 10 |
| **BASIC RHYTHMS** | 11 |
| **GETTING ACQUAINTED WITH TABLATURE** | 12 |
|    Other Notation | 12 |
|    Neck Diagrams | 12 |
| **START MAKING MUSIC!** | 13 |
|    Right-Hand Position | 13 |
|    ● Mini Guitar Lesson: Summary of the Right-Hand Position | 13 |
|    Basic Finger Position | 13 |
|    The Thumb (*p*) Free Stroke (*Tirando*) | 14 |
|    Introducing Low A and Low E (The Open 5th and 6th Strings) | 14 |
|    Left-Hand Position | 15 |
|    Introducing Low B and Low C on the 5th String | 16 |
|    Introducing Low F and Low G on the 6th String | 17 |
|    Introducing Low D, Middle E, and Middle F on the 4th String | 18 |
| **HOW TO PRACTICE** | 19 |
| **PIECES ON THE 4TH AND 5TH STRINGS** | 20 |
|    *Variation on a Melody by Fernando Sor* | 20 |
|    *A Melody from Canarios*, Sanz | 20 |
| **PIECES ON THE 6TH, 5TH, AND 4TH STRINGS** | 21 |
|    *An English Volt* | 21 |
|    *Greensleeves* | 21 |
|    ● Mini Music Lesson: Eighth Note Review | 22 |
|    *Excerpt from Adagio, Opus 15 (duet)*, Giuliani | 22 |
| **FREE STROKE (TIRANDO) WITH *i* AND *m*** | 23 |
|    Two-Note Chords | 23 |
|    Introducing Notes on the 3rd, 2nd, and 1st Strings | 24 |
|    Crossing Strings | 25 |
|    *Aria (duet)* | 26 |
| **INTRODUCING TIES** | 28 |
| **INTRODUCING DOTTED NOTES** | 29 |
|    ● Mini Music Lesson: 6/8 Time | 29 |
|    Introducing High F and G on the 1st String | 30 |
| **INTRODUCING ACCIDENTALS (Sharps ♯, Flats ♭, and Naturals ♮)** | 31 |
|    ● Mini Music Lesson: Accidental Signs | 31 |
|    *Theme from the Fugue in A Minor*, Bach | 32 |
|    *Theme from Lagrima*, Tarrega | 32 |
|    *Theme from Forlorn Hope Fancy*, Dowland | 32 |
| **ALTERNATING BETWEEN THUMB AND FINGERS USING FREE STROKES** | 33 |
| **PIECES WITH THUMB AND TWO-NOTE CHORD ALTERNATIONS** | 34 |
|    *Country Dance No. 1* | 34 |
|    *Homage to Villa-Lobos* | 34 |
|    *In the Style of Leo Brouwer* | 35 |
| **INCOMPLETE MEASURES AND PICKUP NOTES** | 36 |
|    *Grazioso (duet)*, Giuliani | 36 |
|    *Excerpt from Terpsichore (duet)*, Ferrer | 38 |
| **SHIFTING UP THE NECK** | 39 |
|    ● Mini Guitar Lesson: Fret Markers | 39 |
|    ● Mini Guitar Lesson: Positions | 39 |
|    *Spanish Romance*, Traditional | 42 |
|    *Theme from FUGA, BWV 1000*, Bach | 42 |
| **ALTERNATING *p* WITH INDIVIDUAL FINGER STROKES** | 43 |
|    ● Mini Music Lesson: Introducing Sixteenth Notes | 45 |
|    *Theme from Asturias (Leyenda)*, Albéniz | 45 |
|    *Theme from Malagueña*, Traditional Flamenco | 46 |
| **INTRODUCING REST STROKE (APOYANDO)** | 47 |
|    The Position | 47 |
|    The Stroke | 48 |
|    Rest Stroke Alternation | 49 |
|    Alternating *p* with Rest Strokes | 51 |
| **THE MAJOR SCALE** | 52 |
|    Good vs. Bad Crosses | 53 |
| **PLAYING MAJOR SCALES ON ONE STRING: SHIFTING** | 54 |
|    Introducing High A, B, C, D, and E on the 1st String | 56 |
| **PIECES USING REST STROKE AND *p*** | 58 |
|    *Sakura*, Traditional Japanese Melody | 58 |
|    Introducing the Dotted Eighth, Sixteenth Rhythm | 58 |
|    *Variation on a Minuet by José Ferrer* | 58 |
| **CHORDS AND ARPEGGIOS** | 60 |
|    Arpeggios | 61 |
| **ARPEGGIO STUDIES FROM GUILIANI'S 120 RIGHT-HAND STUDIES** | 62 |
| **INTRODUCING TRIPLETS** | 62 |
| **INTRODUCING DYNAMICS** | 63 |
|    Three-Note Chords with *i–m–a* | 64 |
|    The *p–i–m–a* and *p–a–m–i* Arpeggios | 65 |
|    More Arpeggio Studies | 66 |
| **INTRODUCING TEMPO SIGNS** | 67 |
| **SUPPLEMENTAL PIECES** | 67 |
|    *Variation on a Study by Dionisio Aguado* | 67 |
|    Key Signatures | 68 |
|    *Largo from the Concerto in D Major*, Vivaldi | 68 |
|    ● Mini Music Lesson: More Dynamic Signs | 69 |
|    *Lullaby*, Brahms | 70 |
|    *Country Dance*, Carulli | 71 |
|    *Minuet in G*, Bach | 72 |
|    ● Mini Guitar Lesson: Three- and Four-Note Chords | 73 |
|    ● Mini Music Lesson: Introducing the Sixteenth Rest | 73 |
|    *Humoresque*, Dvořák | 74 |
|    *Eine kleine Nachtmusik: Romanze*, Mozart | 76 |
| **DROP D AND G TUNING** | 78 |
|    *Excerpt from Maple Leaf Rag*, Joplin | 78 |
|    *Piano Concerto No. 3, Movement 1 (Theme)*, Beethoven | 80 |

# INTRODUCTION

When I set out to write this book, I wanted to create the most usable and enjoyable classical guitar method available. Having used a number of other methods, my goal was to avoid these pitfalls found in some other methods:

1. The music provided for absolute beginners is usually uninteresting.
2. Notes outside of the first few frets of the fingerboard are too often ignored until too late in the training, the result being many "advanced" students without a thorough knowledge of their own instrument.

*Alfred's Teach Yourself to Play Classical Guitar* is perfect for you if you have no other motivation for learning the guitar than a love of the instrument and an appreciation of its music. This book gives you great pieces to play right away, which keeps learning fun and exciting. Right from the beginning, with limited techniques, you will be playing melodies by Fernando Sor, Mauro Giuliani, J. S. Bach, Gaspar Sanz, and a variety of anonymous Renaissance pieces including "Greensleeves." You will quickly learn notes in upper positions and basic scales at a good pace in a step-by-step manner that will keep your learning enjoyable. As you become more advanced, having this foundation will support your growth as a guitarist and musician. It can be hard to maintain your excitement about making music on the guitar while contending with dry, technical exercises, but with this book, there is always something fun to play.

I wish you lots of joy in your exploration of classical guitar. Also, when you feel ready (certainly, the minute you finish this book and video), I strongly urge you to seek out a good teacher. Find someone who has made classical guitar their specialty and has had plenty of formal training. No book can substitute for the guidance, feedback, and encouragement a good teacher can provide.

If you are a teacher, don't be put off by this book's title! It will work well for giving a beginner a solid start on the instrument without unduly testing their patience with dry, uninteresting, unmusical lessons.

If you have selected this book to use with your beginning students, I thank you for honoring those of us who worked hard to publish it. I know you will interpret the information provided here in light of your own training, and may even use the book in a different order than presented. In any case, it is my sincere wish that you find it a useful tool in your work. Teaching music is a marvelous act of sharing, and we are all fortunate, teachers and students alike, to take part in it.

**Acknowledgements**
With deep appreciation, I would like to thank: for inspiration, instruction, guidance, and encouragement in my formative years, Ray Chester and the late Aaron Shearer; for their support and invaluable help with this book, Ron Manus, Link Harnsberger, and everyone else at Alfred Publishing; for modeling for the drawings in this book, Hector Corrada; for making the drawings, Phil Roberts; for proofreading and just putting up with me in general, my wife, Amy; and for being the light of my life, my daughter, Anna.

## PARTS OF THE GUITAR

A classical guitar has six nylon strings (the lower, thicker three have a light metal wrap over a nylon core). It is lightly constructed for maximum volume. The soundboard is usually constructed of spruce or cedar, and the back and sides are usually rosewood. The fretboard is most often made from a dark hardwood, such as ebony, and the back of the neck mohagany or Spanish Cedar. Other woods are sometimes used, but these are the most common.

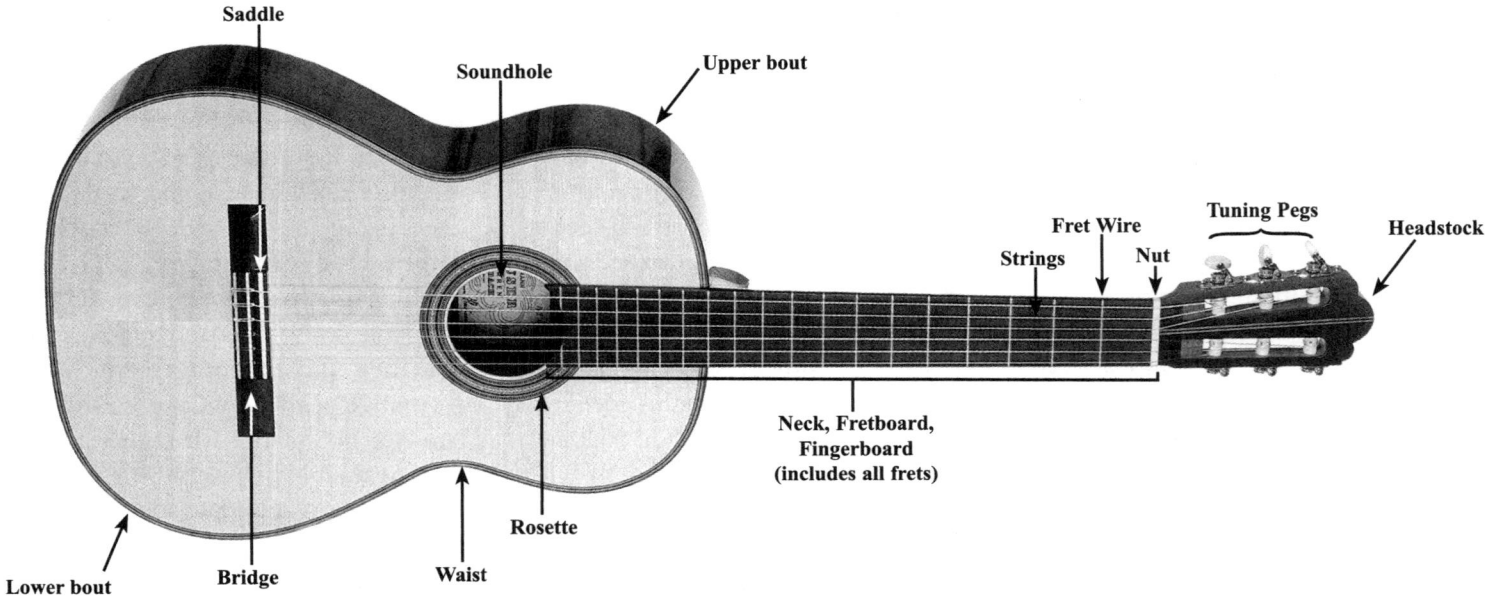

## THE CLASSICAL GUITARIST'S TOOL KIT

Make sure you are equipped with the following items:

- Footstool
- Hard file and nail buffer (or fine grit sandpaper)
- Metronome or metronome app
- Electronic tuner, tuning app, or tuning fork

*Footstool*

*Electronic tuner*

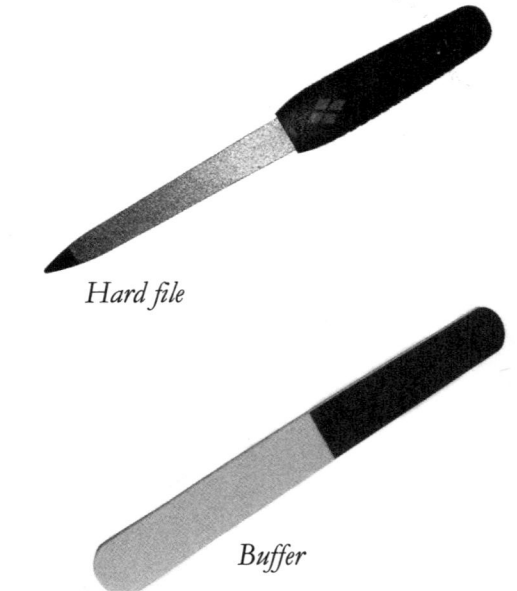

*Hard file*

*Buffer*

*Electronic metronome*

PHOTO BY • Francis Schonken

## TUNING THE GUITAR

There are many ways to tune a guitar. While it is possible to simply use an electronic tuner, it is important to develop your *sense of pitch* (the ability to discern one musical sound from another). Using an electronic tuner at first can help you learn to hear pitch. Make sure to learn at least one of the two methods offered here.

Method No. 1
The strings of the guitar correlate to these notes on the piano.

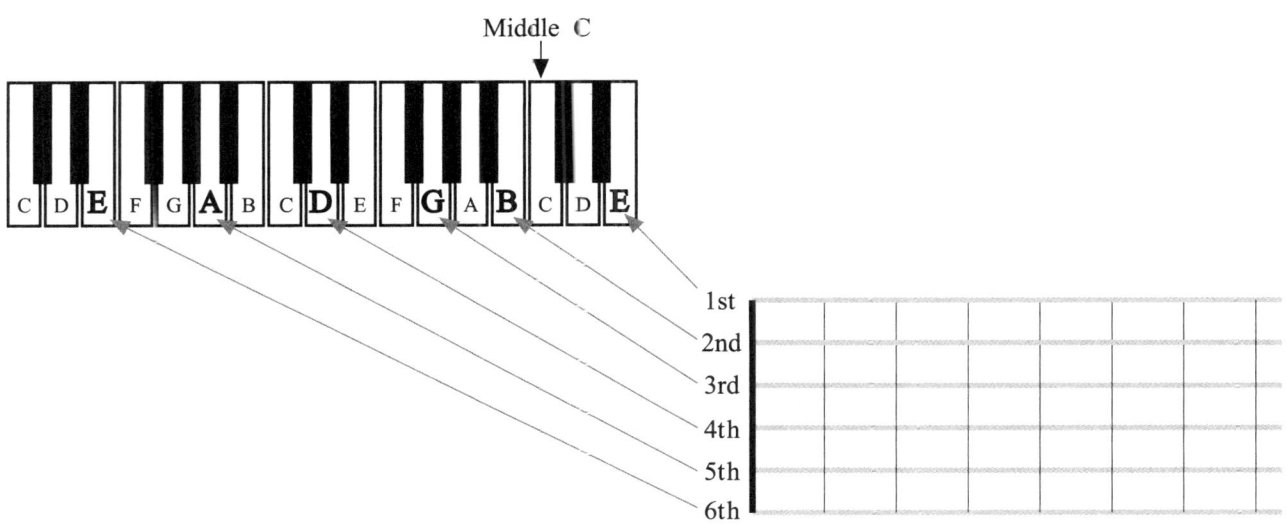

Simply compare the sound of each guitar string to the appropriate piano key, and slowly turn the correct tuning peg until the pitch of the guitar string matches that of the piano. It is best to tune the string low, and then slowly tune it up to pitch. Always listen to the string vibrate as you turn the tuning peg to make sure you don't turn it too far. If you don't have a piano at hand, you can tune to the tuning notes on the video or audio that comes with this book.

 Track 1

Method No. 2
Using the piano (see the piano diagram above), an E tuning fork, another instrument, or an electronic tuner, tune the 6th string to E. Then, tune the 5th string to the 6th, the 4th to the 5th, the 3rd to the 4th, and so on, as illustrated in the diagram below.

Press 5th fret of 6th string to get pitch of 5th string (A).

Press 5th fret of 5th string to get pitch of 4th string (D).

Press 5th fret of 4th string to get pitch of 3rd string (G).

Press 4th fret of 3rd string to get pitch of 2nd string (B).

Press 5th fret of 2nd string to get pitch of 1st string (E).

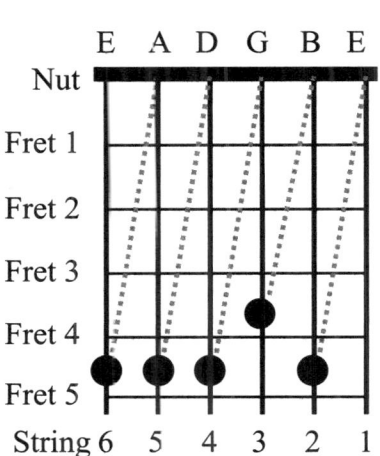

This method is best because you can use it any time—even during a performance!

## THE HANDS

We use our left-hand fingers to play the notes on the neck, and our right-hand fingers to strike the strings. You should become familiar with the names of the fingers and their *joints*. Every finger has three joints, and we use them in very specific ways.

Notice the thumb (*p*) is slightly different than the other fingers as it does not have a knuckle joint.

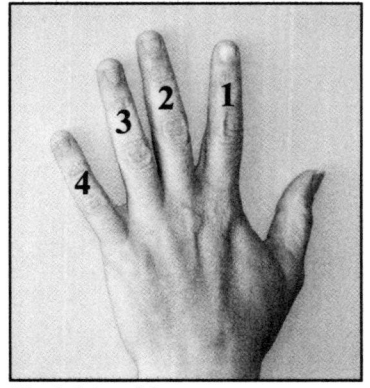
*The left-hand fingers.*

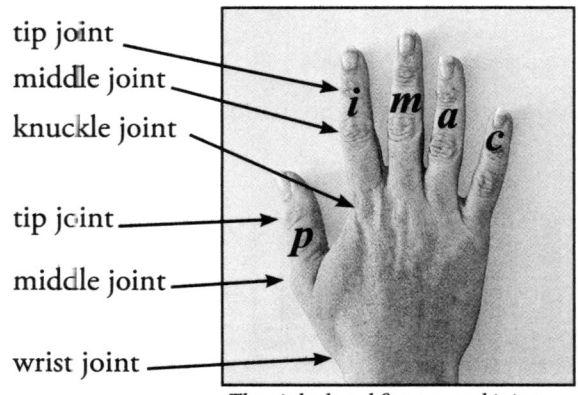
*The right-hand fingers and joints.*

| | | |
|---|---|---|
| *p* = | *pulgar* = | thumb |
| *i* = | *indice* = | index |
| *m* = | *medio* = | middle |
| *a* = | *annular* = | ring finger |
| *c* = | *chiquito* = | pinkie |

### Left-Handed Players

Some left-handed players choose to reverse the functions of the hands and the position of the guitar. This is a personal decision. Lots of left-handed players play conventionally. If you choose to reverse your guitar, you will need to reverse all the instructions in this book (right for left, etc.).

## FINGERNAILS

Classical guitarists use the fingernails of the right hand to strike the strings. As you progress, you will develop a fine sense for just how to place the nails on the strings.

It is very important for you to grow the nails of your right-hand fingers and keep them healthy, clean, smooth, and correctly shaped. They are your tools for playing, just as the violin bow is for the violinist, or the reed is for the clarinetist.

The two drawings below show common lengths and shapes for the thumb nail and the fingers.

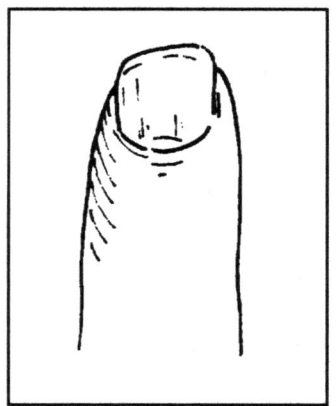

or

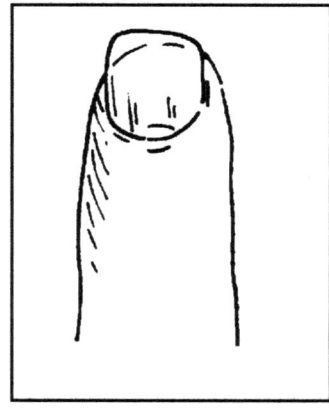

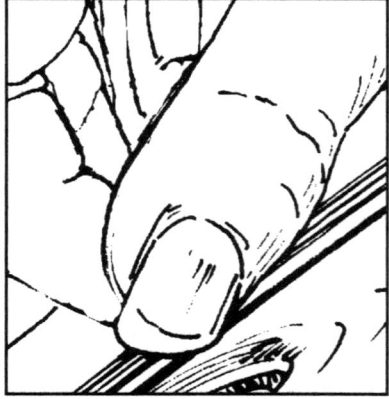

Use a hard file like the one pictured on page 4 to shape the nail. Then, use either a buffer or "wet-or-dry" 600 grit sandpaper to bring the edge of each nail to a high polish. They should be absolutely smooth! Nicks and bumps in the nails cause scratchy, unattractive sounds. It's not too soon to start caring for these very important tools.

## SEATING POSITION

If you have ever seen a classical guitarist play, you know that we sit while we play and that our position is unique among guitarists. The position has developed over centuries of guitar playing and experimentation. While each guitarist is unique, and therefore sits slightly differently from others, the following four goals we all share lead us to have more in common than not.

**The goals of the seating position:**
1. Minimize tension in the body and hands.
2. Provide easy access to the entire length of the fingerboard.
3. Give easy access to all six strings.
4. Securely support the instrument without the use of the hands.

As you learn proper seating, you may experience some slight discomfort, or feel unsure about it. Just because it doesn't "come naturally" to you doesn't mean it isn't making the best use of your body. Be patient! Be observant of other players, and check your position often.

**Getting Into Position**
Follow these steps and you will be on your way to having a correct seating position.

1. Put a footstool in front of the front left leg of an armless chair with a flat seat.
2. Stand with your feet on either side of the footstool, facing away from the chair. Sit on the very left front-edge of the chair.
3. Place your left foot on the footstool, keeping your leg perpendicular to the floor. Place your right foot and knee out to the right.
4. Place the lower curve of the guitar snugly on your left knee so that:
    a. The upper edge of the back of the guitar is in the center of your chest.
    b. The head of the guitar is eye level, and just barely in front of you.
    c. The right side of the guitar is resting on the inside of your right thigh.
5. Place your right forearm on the outer edge of the guitar, aligned with or just to your right of the bridge, depending on your size.

# TEACH YOURSELF TO PLAY CLASSICAL GUITAR

 ## THE GUITAR FINGERBOARD

The *musical alphabet* has only seven letters. Every *note* or *pitch* (musical sound) has one of these names:

**A  B  C  D  E  F  G**

These seven letter names repeat themselves again and again:

**A  B  C  D  E  F  G  A  B  C**   etc.

The distance between two notes with the same name is called an *octave*. Even though they have the same name, one will be higher or lower sounding than the other.

The distance from one note to the other in the musical alphabet is measured in *steps*. Steps come in two sizes:

---

 **Half Steps and Whole Steps**

**Half step:** A *half step* is the distance from any fret to an adjacent fret. For instance, from the 1st fret to the 2nd fret is one half step. From an open string to the 1st fret is also one half step.

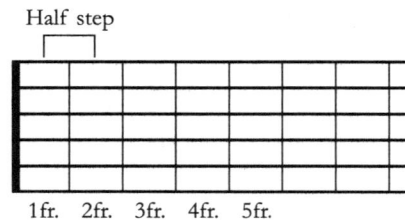

**Whole step:** The distance of two frets is a *whole step*. For instance, from the 1st fret to the 3rd fret is a whole step. From an open string to the 2nd fret is also one whole step.

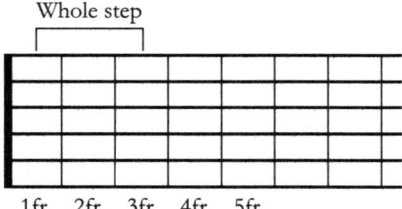

# READING MUSIC: PITCH

## Notes

Musical sounds are indicated by symbols called *notes*. Their time value is determined by their color (white or black) and by stems and flags attached to the note.

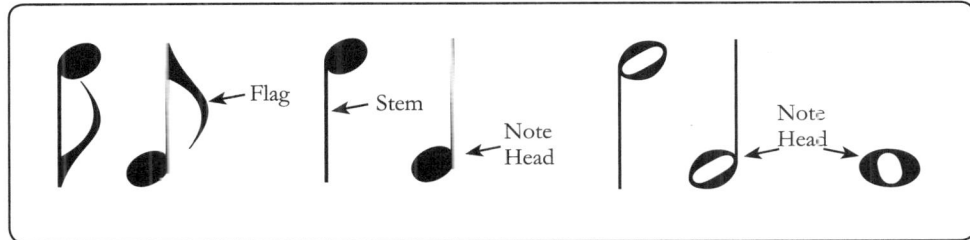

## The Staff

The name and *pitch* (degree of highness or lowness) of the notes are determined by the note's position on a graph made of five horizontal lines, and the spaces in between, called the *staff*. The notes are named after the first seven letters of the alphabet (A–G), repeated to embrace the entire range of musical sound.

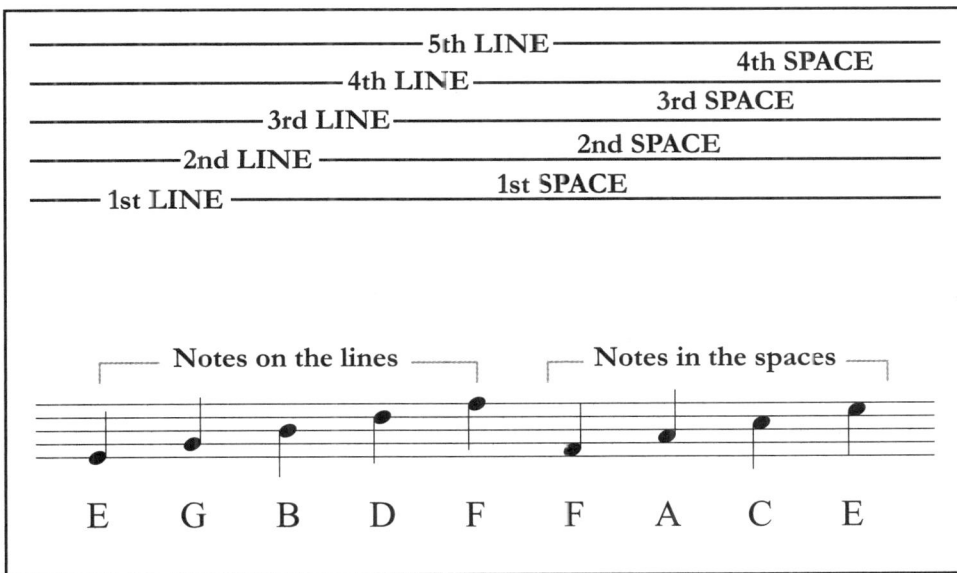

## Clefs

During the evolution of musical notation, the staff had from 2 to 20 lines, and symbols were invented to locate certain lines and the pitch of the note on that line. These symbols are called *clefs*. Music for guitar is written in the *G clef,* or *treble clef*.

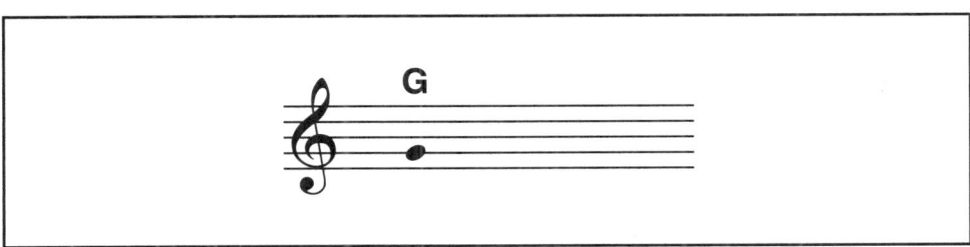

Two other devices will help you memorize the line and space notes. The phrase **E**very **G**ood **B**oy **D**oes **F**ine will help you remember the line note names, from low to high: E, G, B, D, F. The word **FACE** contains the space note names from low to high.

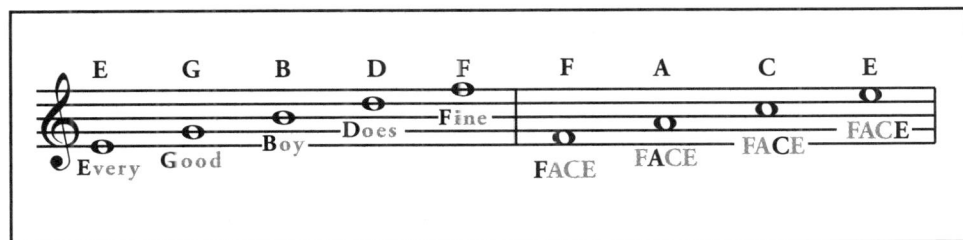

The higher or lower a note is written on the staff, the higher or lower it sounds. Notes below and above the staff have *ledger lines*. Ledger line notes are easy to read, since they each look very different from all the others.

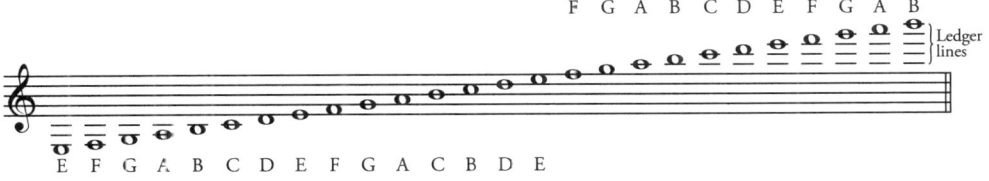

## GETTING STARTED: READING MUSIC: TIME

### Note Durations

The location of a note in relation to the staff tells us its pitch. The duration, or *value*, is indicated by its shape.

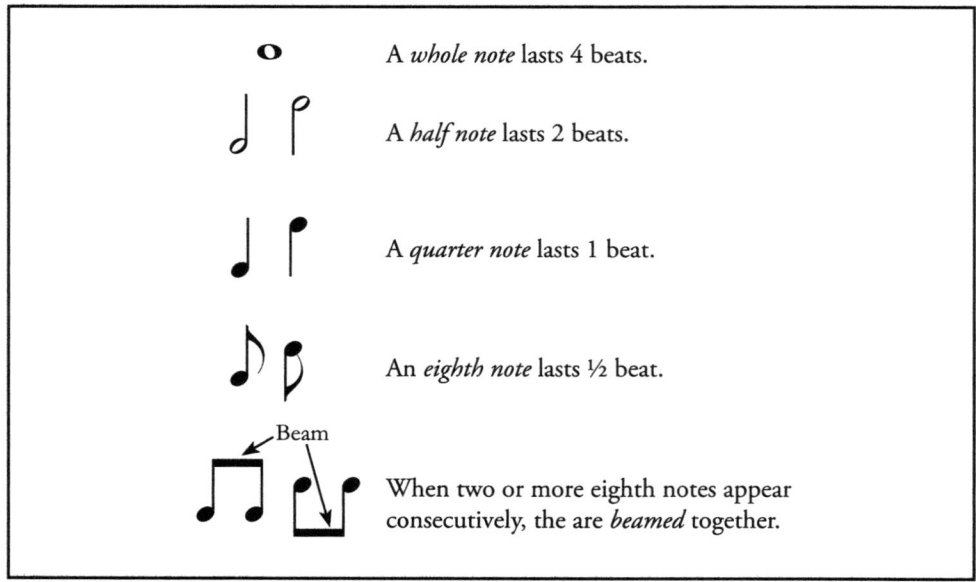

### Rests

So far we've covered four types of note values. They each have a corresponding duration of silence known as a *rest*. A *whole rest* means four beats of silence, a *half rest* means two beats of silence, and so forth.

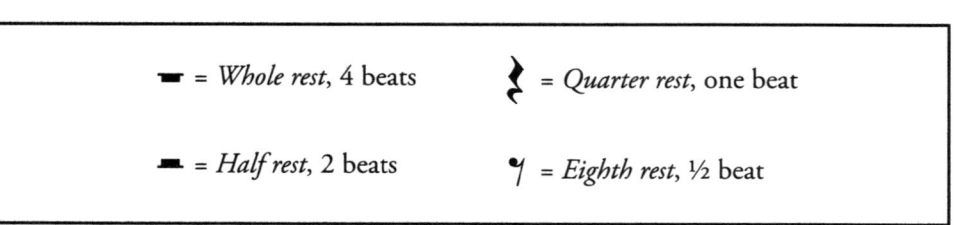

### Measures

*Measures* divide music into groups of *beats*. A beat is an equal division of time. Beats are the basic pulse behind music. The vertical lines that cross through the staff are called *bar lines*. They show where one measure begins and another ends. *Double bars* mark the end of a section or small example.

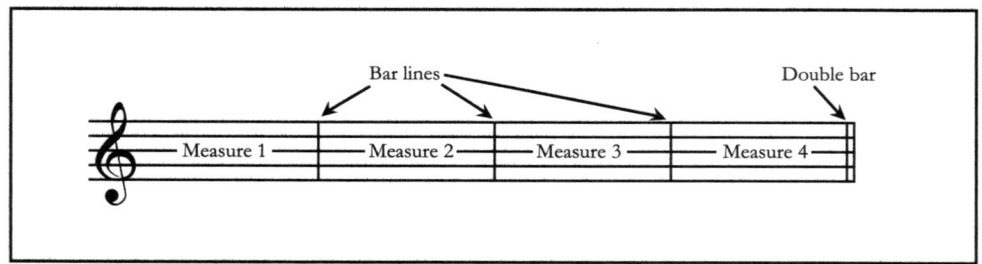

### Time Signatures

At the beginning of any piece you'll find a *time signature*. A time signature consists of two numbers, one on top of the other, which looks similar to a fraction. The top number indicates how many beats are in a measure. The bottom number tells you what kind of note gets one count.

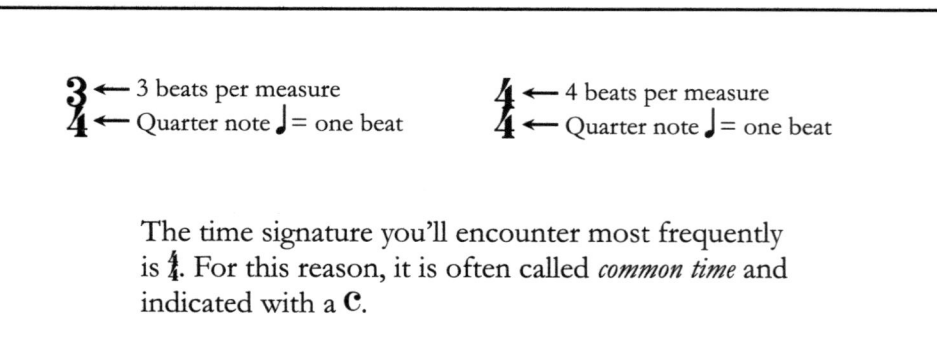

The time signature you'll encounter most frequently is 4/4. For this reason, it is often called *common time* and indicated with a **C**.

## BASIC RHYTHMS

The following exercises will get you familiar with the basic rhythms you just learned. You don't need a guitar.

Count the numbers below the staff out loud as you clap your hands in the rhythm shown. Hold your hands together for the full duration of each note, and hold them apart during the rests. Counting for rests is shown in parentheses. Use a metronome set to a slow *tempo* (speed) such as ♩ = 48. This will help you keep a steady tempo and learn how to evenly fit two eighth notes into the space of one beat.

*Repeat sign.*
This sign indicates that the music should be repeated.

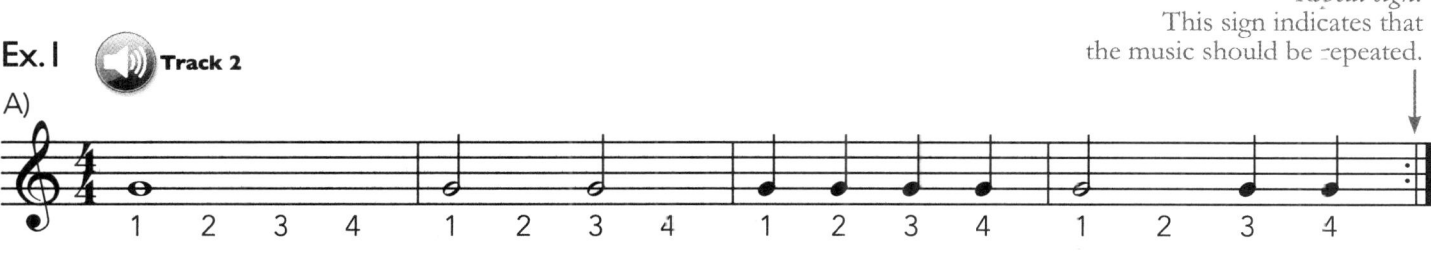

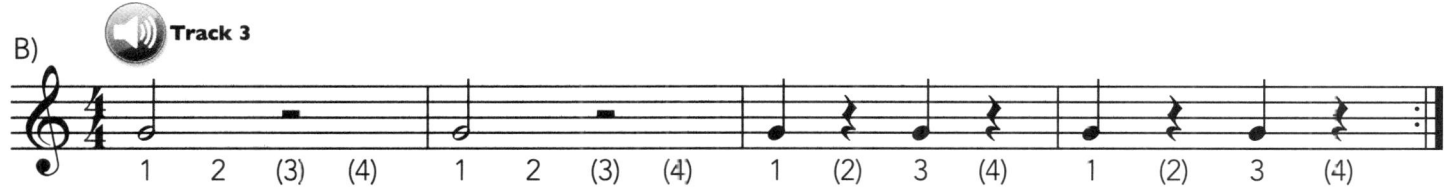

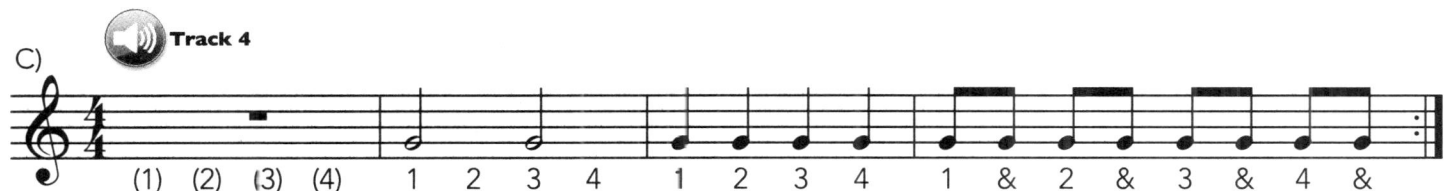

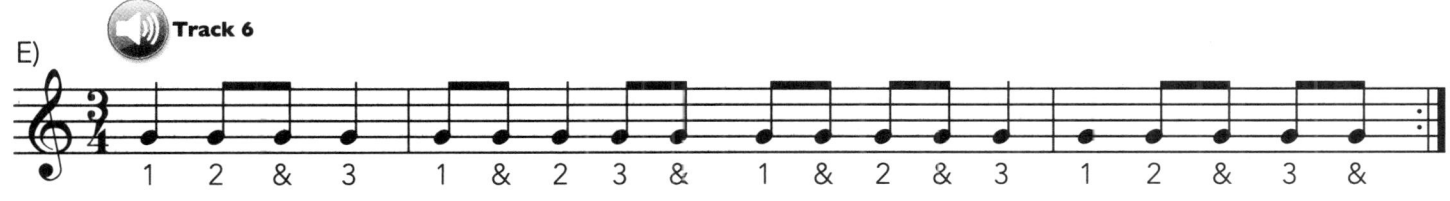

 ## GETTING ACQUAINTED WITH TABLATURE

*Tablature* (TAB) is a graphic method of showing how to play notes and chords on the guitar. It uses a six-line staff, each line representing one string of the guitar.

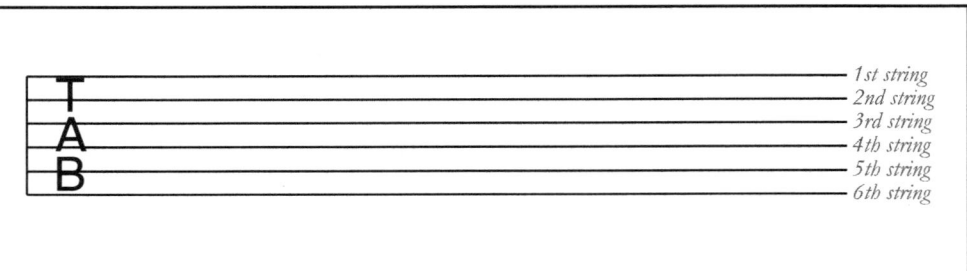

A number placed on a line means to play that fret on the corresponding string. For example,

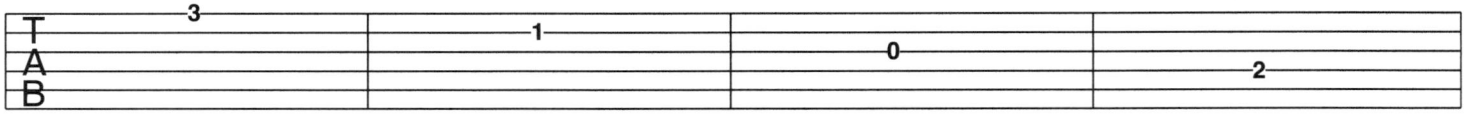

| Play the 1st string, 3rd fret | 2nd string, 1st fret | 3rd string, open | 4th string, 2nd fret |

Numbers placed one on top of the other are played simultaneously.

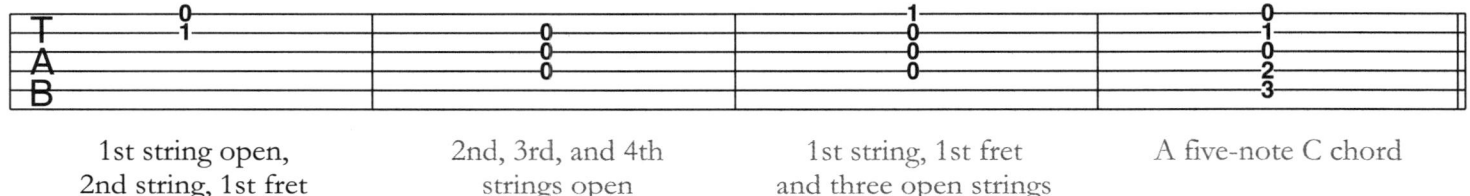

| 1st string open, 2nd string, 1st fret | 2nd, 3rd, and 4th strings open | 1st string, 1st fret and three open strings | A five-note C chord |

## Other Notation

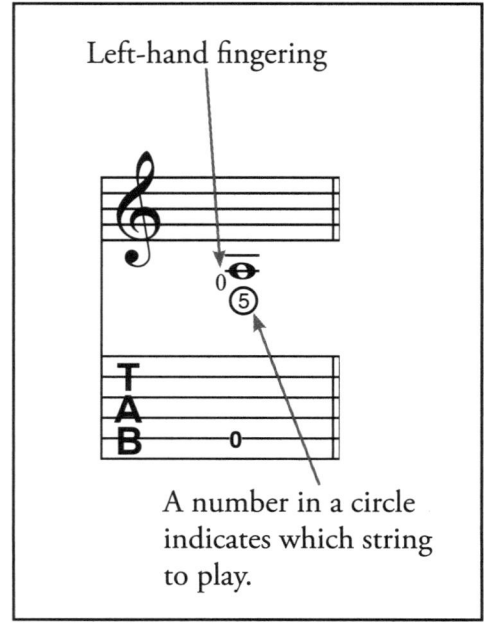

A number in a circle indicates which string to play.

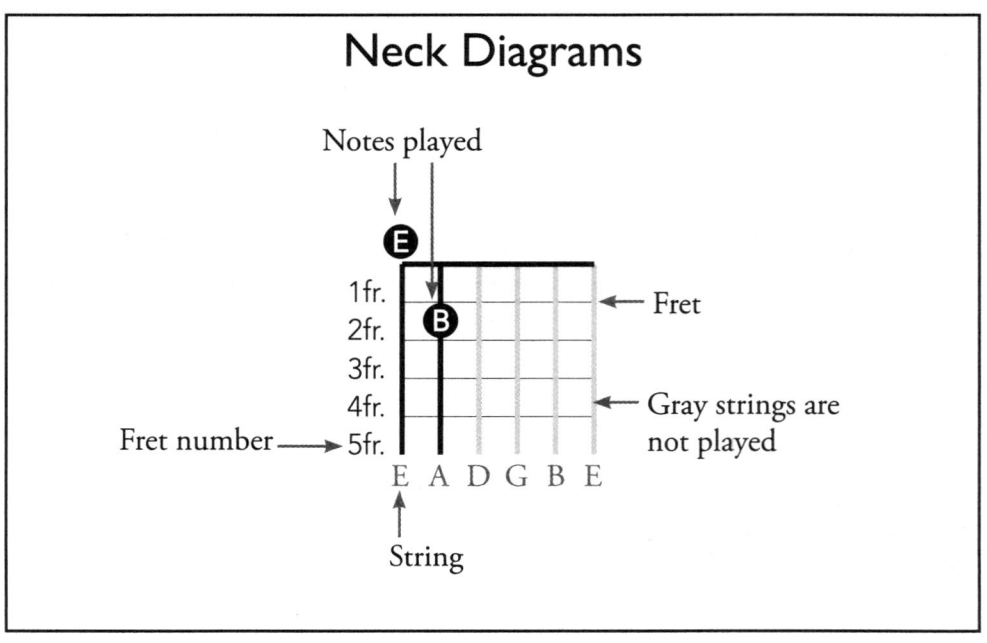

# START MAKING MUSIC!

To produce a musical sound from your guitar, you will need to develop a good technique for striking the strings. The most fundamental aspect of striking the strings is the right-hand position.

## Right-Hand Position

The muscles that control the fingers are attached at their ends to the elbow joint and pass through the wrist on their way to the fingers. Since we are always concerned about making guitar playing as easy and stress-free as possible, we want to avoid pulling on these muscles unnecessarily. For that reason, it's important to keep your wrist straight (aligned with the arm). Use a mirror to observe your wrist position.

We need room to operate the fingers freely, so arch the wrist very slightly, so that the top of the wrist is just further from the soundboard than the knuckle joints. Do not overdo this! Your wrist should be almost flat. Bending your wrist too much can cause serious problems.

The two fingers we use most, *i* (index) and *m* (middle), are of different lengths: *i* is shorter than *m* for almost everybody, so rotate or tilt the arm towards *i* (on an axis that runs through *m* to the elbow) so that you can just barely see the knuckle of your *a* (ring) finger when you look down at your hand. Not only will this help to equalize the length of *i* and *m*, but it will help you play on the left side of your nail, and simplify your thumb stroke, too.

**Summary of the Right-Hand Position**

- Straight wrist — Use a mirror to check.
- Arch — The top of your wrist should be slightly further out from the soundboard than your knuckle joints.
- Tilt — The *a* knuckle joint should be just barely visible when you look down at your hand.

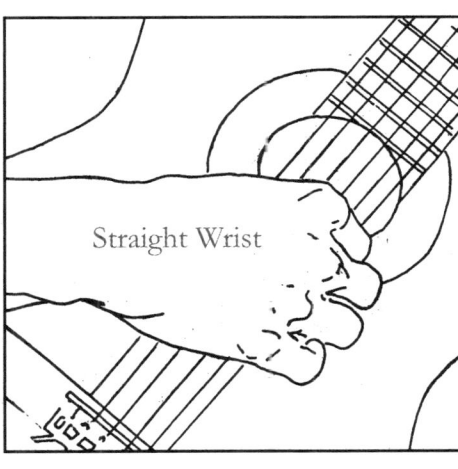
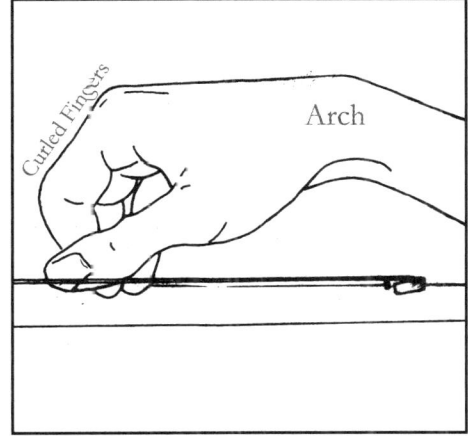
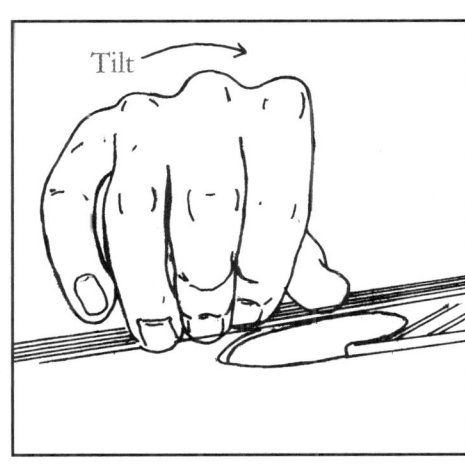

## Basic Finger Position

Being careful to position your arm and wrist correctly, place *i* and *m* on the 2nd and 3rd strings, respectively. Move your arm and hand so that your fingers are slightly curled. Your *i* finger, which is positioned on the 3rd string, should be positioned so its middle joint is curled above the 2nd string. The *m* finger, which is on the 2nd string, will be positioned so its middle joint is curled above the 1st string. The other fingers, *a* and *c* (pinkie), will also be lightly curled. Your thumb, *p*, should rest lightly against the tip of *i*. The overall effect should be that of a loosely held fist...as if you were holding a ball.

## The Thumb (*p*) Free Stroke (*Tirando*)

As you begin playing with your thumb (*p*), strive for a clear, strong *tone*. Tone refers to the quality of the sound you make—one of the most important considerations in learning to play classical guitar.

For now, rest *i* and *m* on the 3rd (G) and 2nd (B) strings respectively. Let's begin by playing the open 5th string (A).

### The Three-Step Thumb Stroke

There are three steps to a good *p* stroke: extend, prepare, and follow-through. Starting from an at-rest position (resting against the tip of the *i* finger):

1. Gracefully and smoothly *extend* (move away from the palm) *p* from the wrist and tip joints. The wrist joint does most of the work. Don't work the middle joint at all.
2. Prepare *p* on the 5th string so that the nail and flesh are both touching the string. Your tip should not extend any further than is needed to get the nail on the string. For most of us, the tip joint will appear very slightly *flexed* (bent towards the palm) when we are on the string. Be careful *not* to overextend the tip, as if you were hitchhiking.
3. Dig into the string with the tip joint, supporting and pushing from the wrist joint, then floppily and freely follow through into the tip joint of *i*. Avoid any extra, circular motions.

## Introducing Low A and Low E (The Open 5th and 6th Strings)

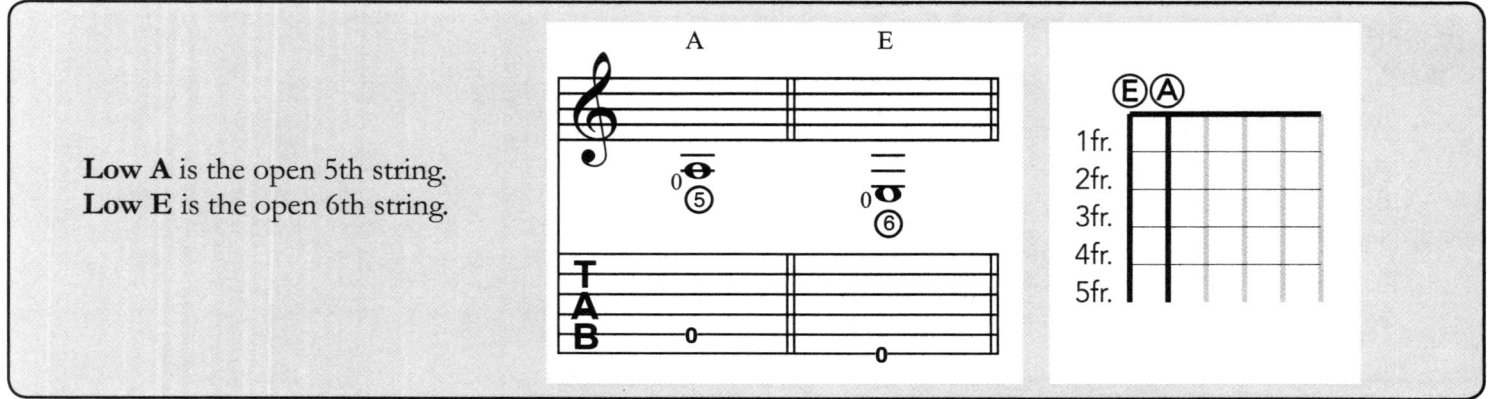

**Low A** is the open 5th string.
**Low E** is the open 6th string.

Practice these introductory exercises very slowly, being careful to execute the three-step thumb stroke described above.

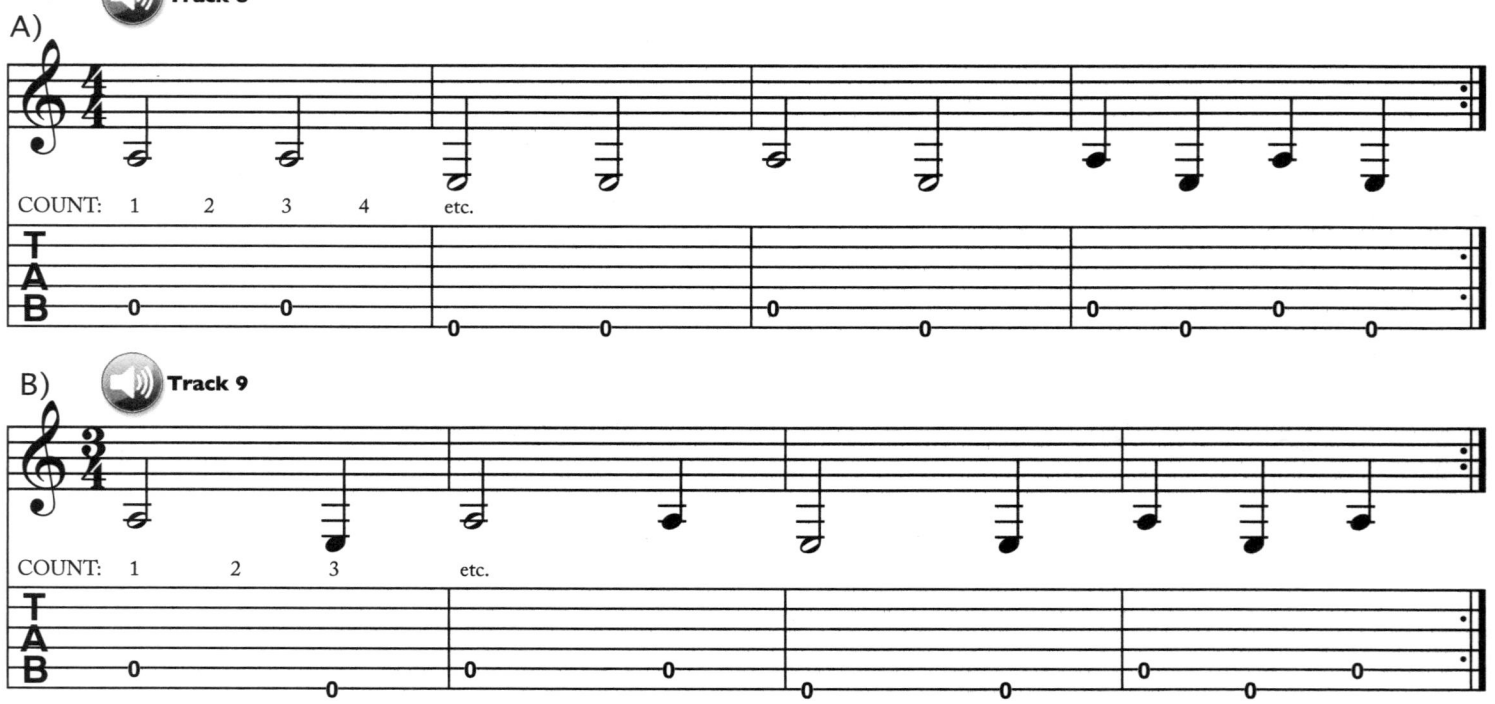

# LEFT-HAND POSITION

The ideas behind the left-hand position are similar to those for the right-hand position. Your wrist should be aligned with your arm. The arch of your wrist should be minimal.

Place your thumb behind the neck, just under your 2nd finger.

Let's place all four left-hand fingers on the first four frets. Your 1st finger should be placed well to the left side of the fingertip and the 2nd finger just slightly so. The 3rd finger should be placed on the center of the fingertip, and your 4th finger will touch the string on its right side.

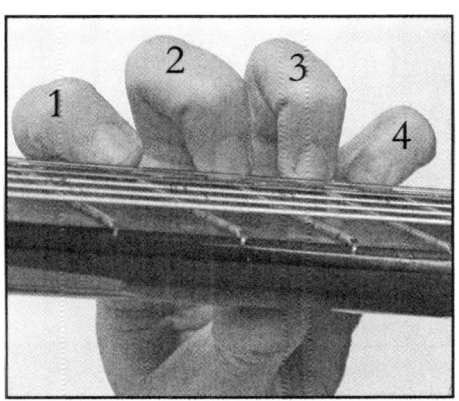

Notice that in the photo above, the fingers are very gently curled. It is not necessary to play on the very tips of the fingers all the time. For now, play a little bit below the very end of the finger, well away from the fingernails (which should be very short). Remember to always avoid extremes of flexion or extension when positioning the hands and fingers.

The fingers should always touch the strings just to the left of the frets, as close as possible to the fret wire without being on top of it. If you are too far from the fret, unattractive buzzes will result. If you are too far on top of the fret, the notes will sound muted.

Never press hard! You do not need to press the strings into the wood of the fretboard. You need only secure the string against the fret, thus shortening the vibrating length of the string and changing the pitch.

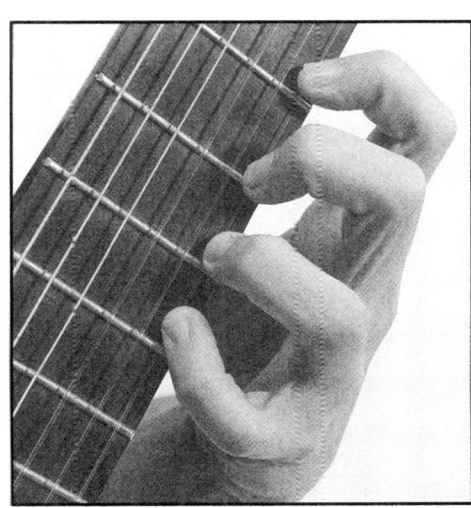

### Fernando Sor

*Born in 1778 and died in 1839, Fernando Sor is considered one of the most important composers for the guitar. Born in Barcelona, Spain, he also resided in London, Moscow, and Paris. He composed over 400 guitar pieces, and in 1827 published his famous guitar method.*

## Introducing Low B and Low C on the 5th String

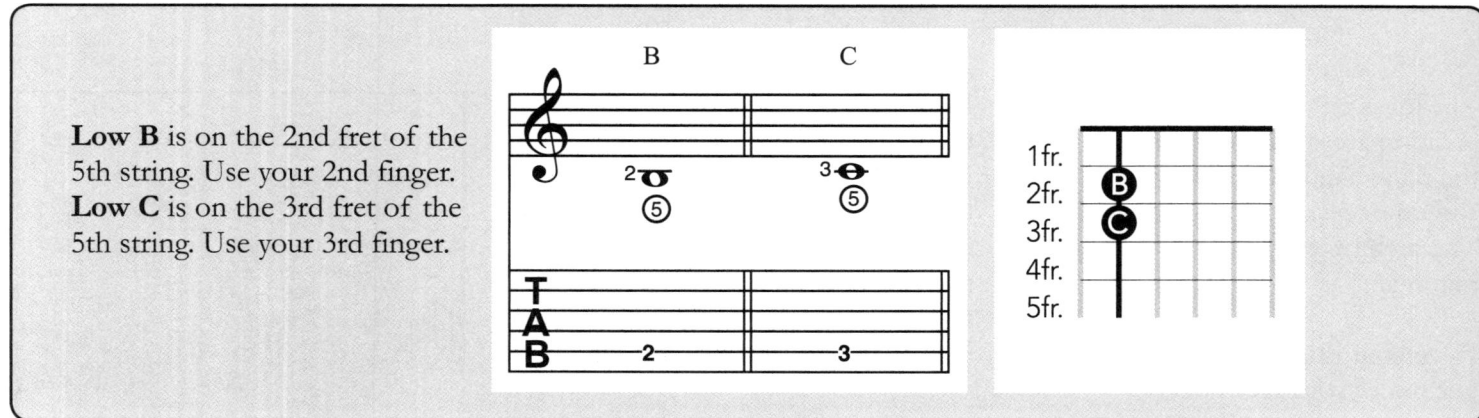

Low B is on the 2nd fret of the 5th string. Use your 2nd finger.
Low C is on the 3rd fret of the 5th string. Use your 3rd finger.

For now, keep *i* and *m* resting on the 3rd and 2nd strings respectively. Check your position frequently to make sure *i* and *m* remain lightly curled.

Pay very close attention to both the right- and left-hand positions as you play these exercises. Remember to always place left-hand fingers directly to the left of the frets. The further from the frets you press, the more difficult it becomes to avoid disagreeable buzzing sounds.

Ex.3  Track 10

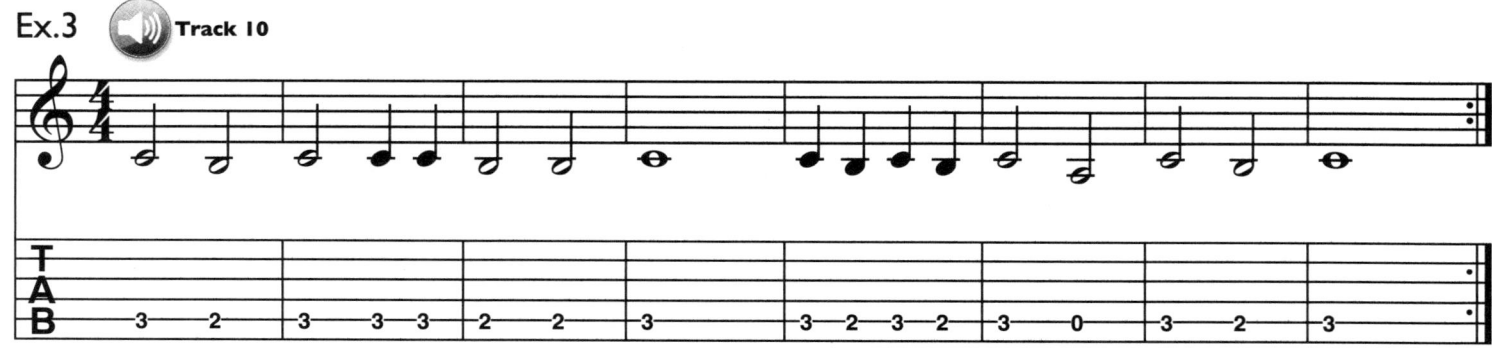

Ex.4  Track 11

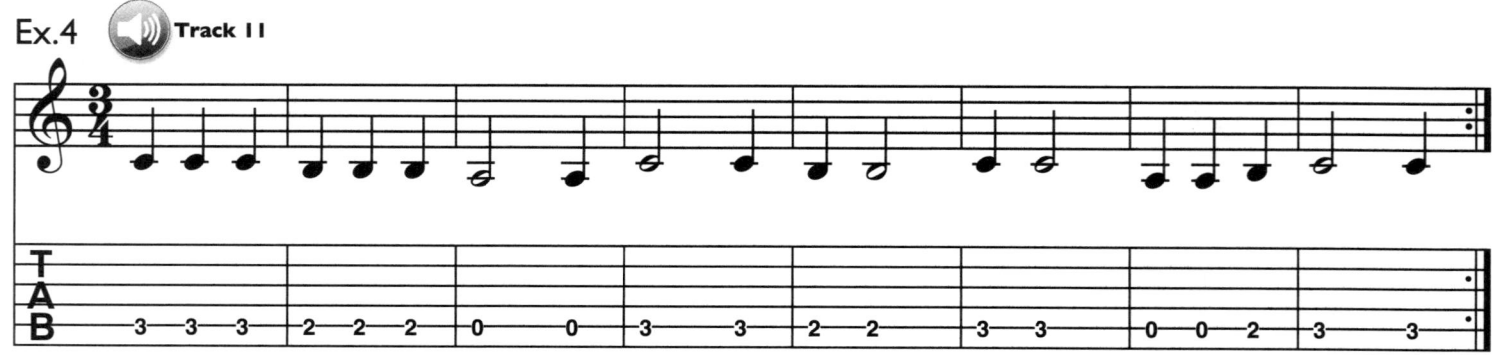

## Introducing Low F and Low G on the 6th String

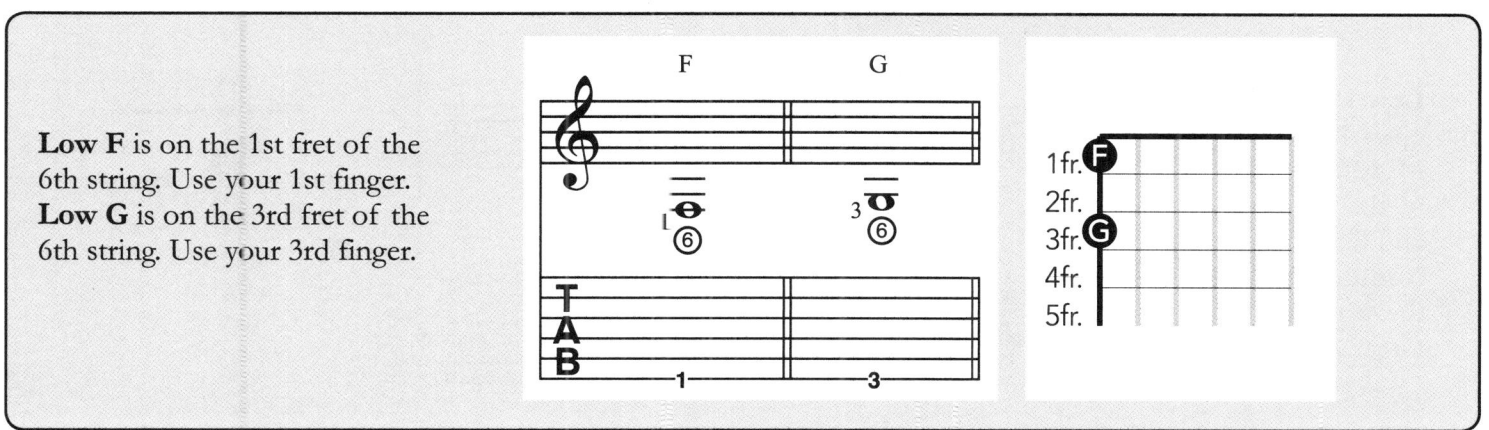

Low F is on the 1st fret of the 6th string. Use your 1st finger.
Low G is on the 3rd fret of the 6th string. Use your 3rd finger.

Ex.5  Track 12

Ex.6  Track 13

## Introducing Low D, Middle E, and Middle F on the 4th String

**Low D** is played on the open 4th string.
**Middle E** is the 2nd fret of the 4th string. Use your 2nd finger.
**Middle F** is the 3rd fret of the 4th string. Use your 3rd finger.

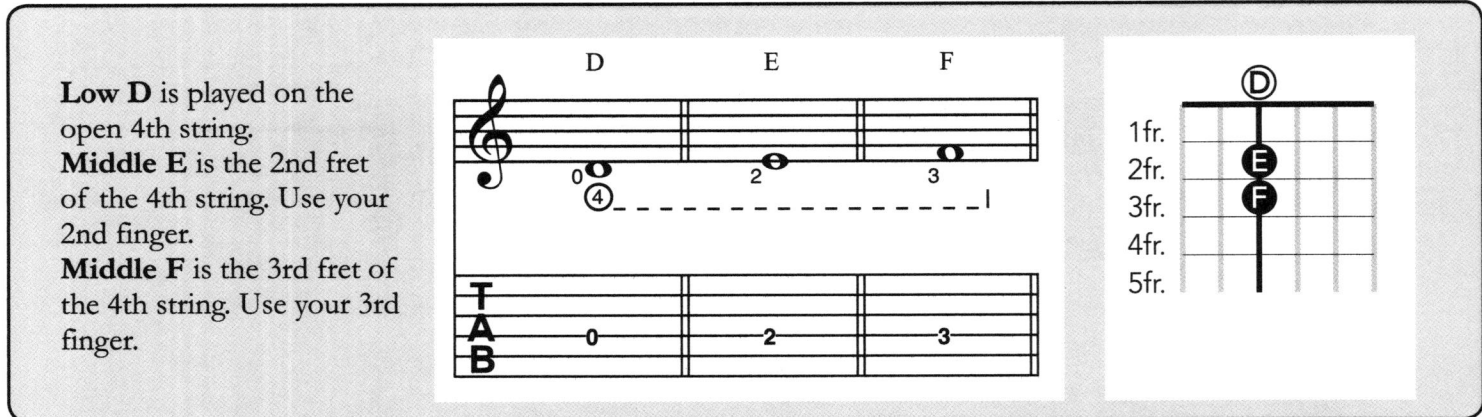

Ex.7  **Track 14**

Continue using the *p* stroke.

Ex.8  **Track 15**

In $\frac{2}{4}$ time, there are two beats per measure and the quarter note gets one beat.

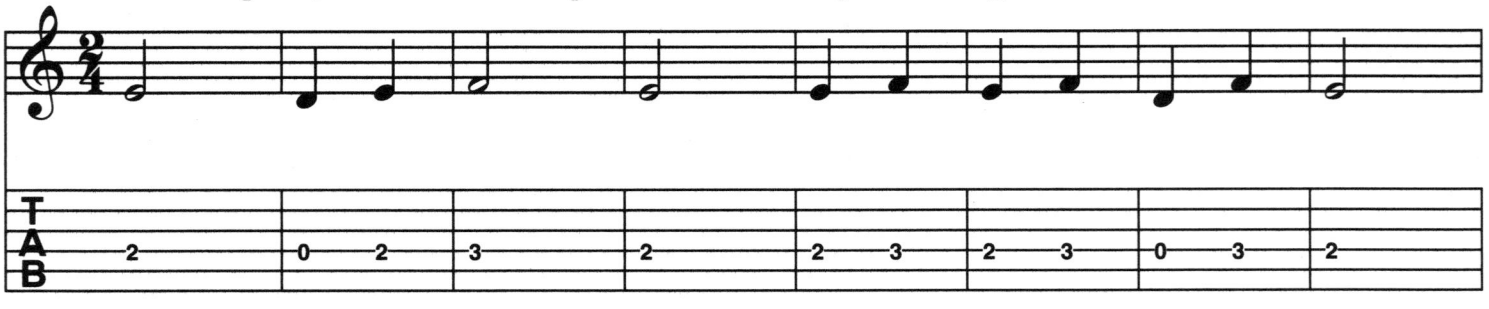

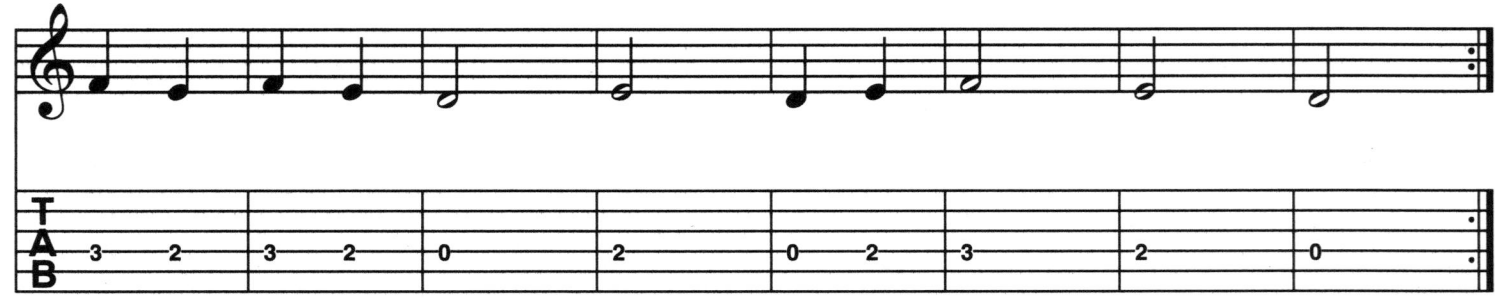

# HOW TO PRACTICE

The most important thing you will ever learn is how to learn! Fulfillment in your life with the guitar can easily become frustration without a good approach to practicing. One cannot learn to play well by practicing poorly. By the same token, you will reach the upward limits of your potential through good, methodical, and regular practice.

**How Long Should You Practice?**
The amount of time you spend will reflect the depth of your interest, and what your aspirations are. If you want to become a great professional concert artist, you will eventually spend many hours each day practicing, especially in your first few years. If you love the guitar but are pursuing it as a hobby, it is a good idea to find one hour a day to practice—although not necessarily in one sitting. It is important that your powers of concentration be at their best when practicing. Even many experts in the art of practicing an instrument find that their concentration wanes after about 20 minutes. Try practicing in three 20-minute sessions, or even four 15-minute sessions. Anyone who really loves the guitar will want to pick it up several times a day for a few minutes, and a lot can be accomplished this way. You may find that your ability to concentrate for longer periods will increase, and, if your schedule allows, the total time that you practice will increase, too.

**Set Goals**
More important than how long you practice, or even what you practice, is *how* you practice. You should always have specific goals for your practice. For instance, "Today, I want to be able to play these two exercises smoothly and with confidence," or "Today I will review everything I did yesterday and learn these two new notes." If you find you're not accomplishing your goals, try setting easier goals. It's important to try to succeed every day. Nothing breeds success like success! If you find yourself reaching your goals before an hour has passed, try setting higher goals for yourself. Never play aimlessly. You're either progressing or regressing. Nothing you do on the guitar is ever neutral, or meaningless.

**Prepare - Repeat - Review**
Everyone eventually establishes their own personal approach to practice. All successful approaches, however, follow a pattern similar to the one given here.

When learning a new piece or exercise, follow these five steps:

- Prepare (Steps 1, 2, and 3)
  **Step 1.** Take a very small portion of the piece, such as two measures, or a short phrase, and familiarize yourself with the rhythms by counting the beats aloud and clapping. Do this very slowly, since you will be playing slowly.
  **Step 2.** Familiarize yourself with the names of the notes in this short portion by pointing at each one and saying its name aloud.
  **Step 3.** Learn the left-hand fingerings in this short portion by pointing at the notes, picturing (visualizing) your left hand playing them on the guitar and saying the finger numbers aloud. Then name the fret numbers.

- Repeat (Step 4)
  **Step 4.** When Steps 1–3 are easy for you, pick up your guitar and begin playing this portion of the piece very slowly. Make sure to play slowly enough to guarantee success; you should be able to think of the note names and visualize the fingerings *before* you play each note. If you are getting confused or making errors—if you feel rushed at all—slow down! Frustration is never fun, anyway. You may find that a metronome, set as slowly as it goes, may help you keep control over the speed at which you play. Repeat the passage as many times as is necessary to feel confident. Usually, confidence comes when something has been done well many times in a row. Your goal here is to develop habits of ease and confidence, and habits are formed through repetition.

- Review (Step 5)
  **Step 5.** Repeat Steps 1–4 with the next small portion of the piece, and then play through all the sections you have learned thus far, until you can play through all of them in succession with confidence. The next day, when you continue your study of the piece, start by playing everything you learned the first day as slowly as possible, until confidence returns. There is always attrition from day to day. In other words, if you master an exercise after an hour of practice today, it won't necessarily be mastered when you wake up tomorrow. It may take a little while to regain that progress. Three steps forward and one step back is normal for many of us. Stay in there! That's why review is so important.

Put this practice method to work as you learn the studies and pieces in this book. Enjoy your success!

## PIECES ON THE 4TH AND 5TH STRINGS

### Variation on a Melody by Fernando Sor

### A Melody from Canarios

by Gaspar Sanz

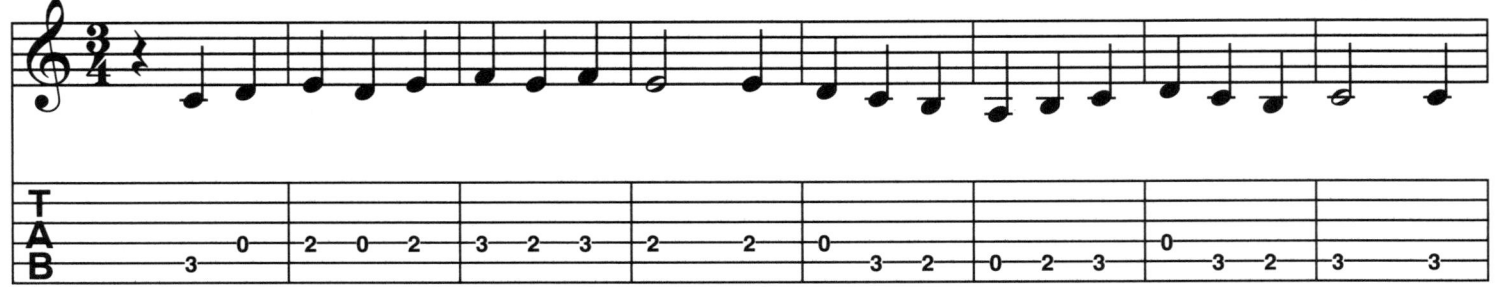

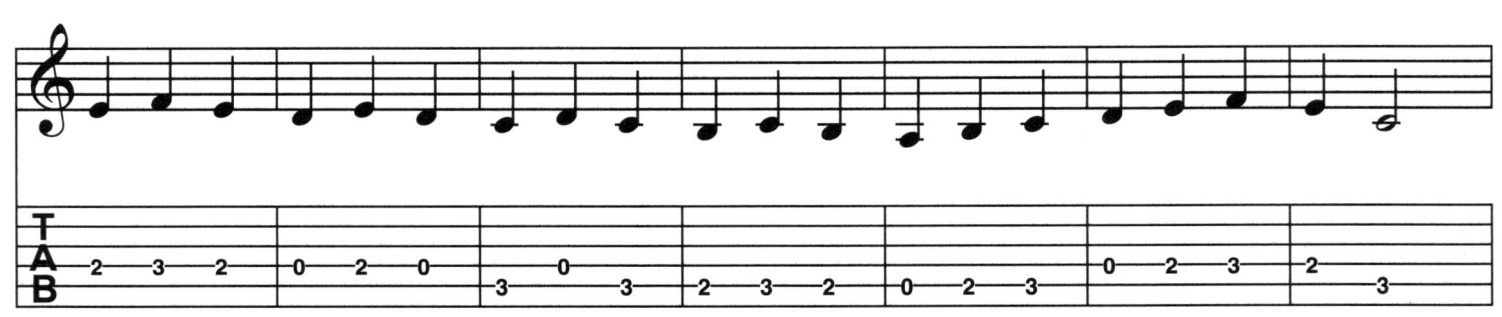

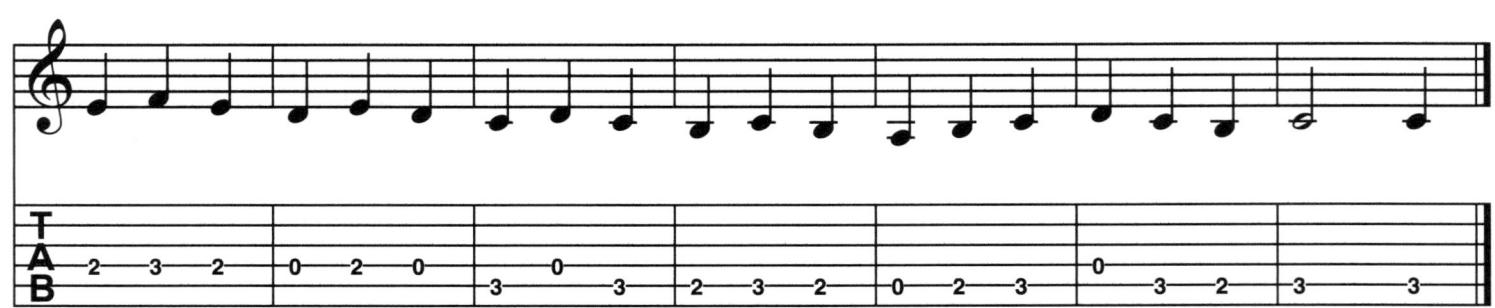

# PIECES ON THE 6TH, 5TH, AND 4TH STRINGS

Play close attention to your *p* strokes. While you should still think in terms of the three-step thumb stroke, you should be striving for a more continuous stroke. Preparing on the string should be more of an idea than an action. In other words, try to pass directly through the string without first stopping the sound of the previous note. Remember to follow through fully. Also, if you feel you are ready, it may be time to try playing without resting *i* and *m* on the strings. Float loosely above the strings, but keep your hand as still as possible. Play firmly, but not too forcefully.

## An English Volt  Track 18

An Elizabethan court dance, the *Volt*, also called *La volta*, *Volta*, or *volte*, was the only dance which allowed the dancers to embrace.

by Anonymous

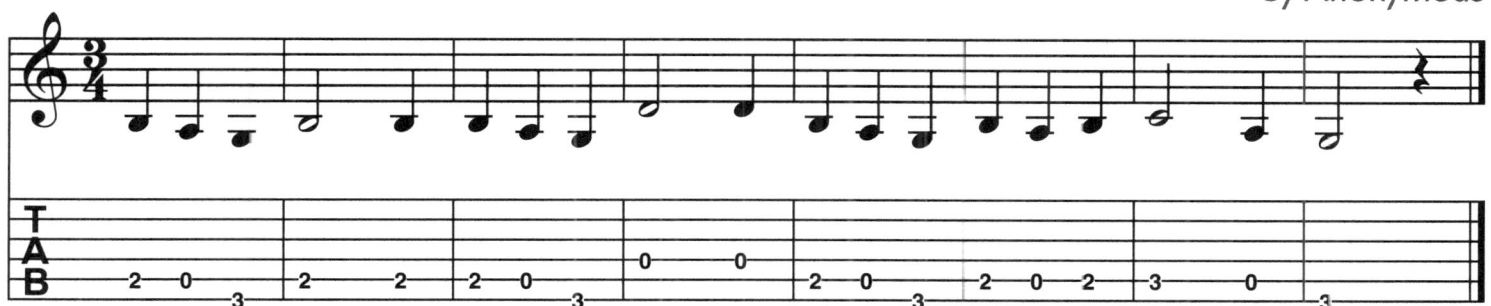

## Greensleeves Track 19

by Anonymous

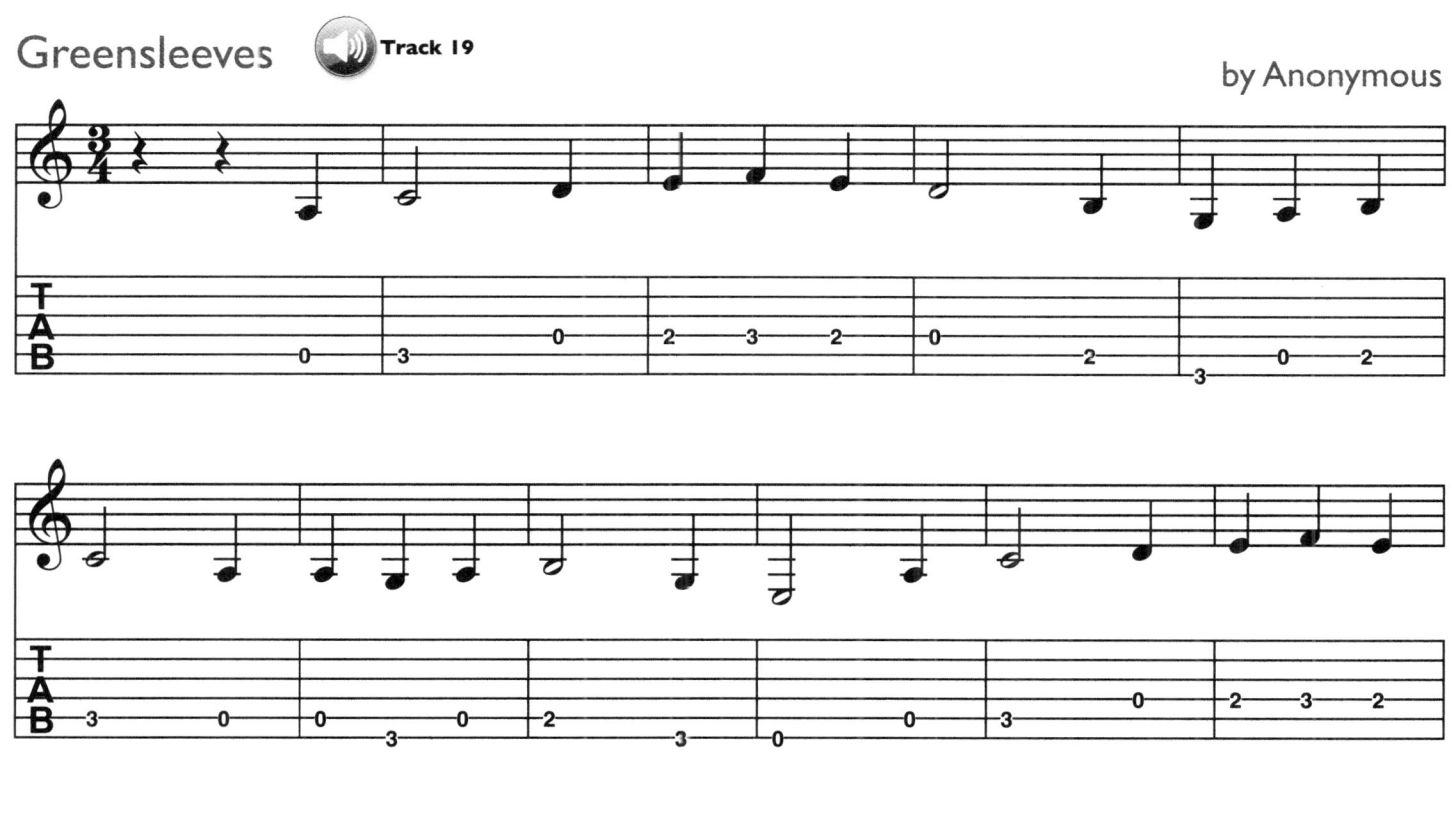

*Excerpt from*
# Adagio, Opus 15 (Duet)

Track 20 Both Parts  Track 21 Accompaniment

This piece has been arranged as a *duet* (a piece for two instruments). You play the music on the lower staff (Student). A friend or teacher can play the top staff, or you can play along with the audio that comes with this book.

Pay close attention to the rests in this piece. They indicate silence, so you will need to stop the vibrating string with *p*. This is called *damping*. Simply touch the string with the fleshy part of *p* at exactly the moment indicated by the rests. For instance, in the second measure, touch the string with *p* exactly on the second beat. Keep in mind that, while it's always important, playing with good rhythm is especially important when playing with others. Count carefully!

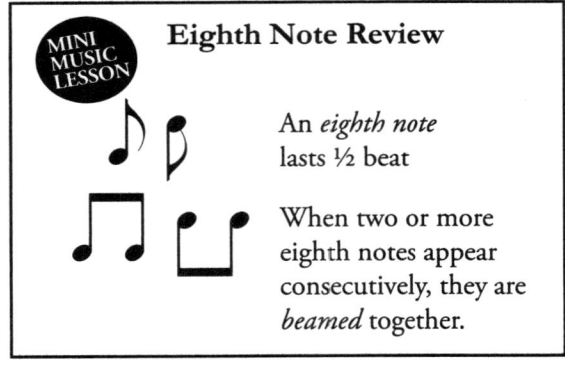

**Eighth Note Review**

An *eighth note* lasts ½ beat

When two or more eighth notes appear consecutively, they are *beamed* together.

by Mauro Giuliani

# FREE STROKE (TIRANDO) WITH *i* AND *m*

## Two-Note Chords

In *free stroke* we strike the strings and then swing freely inward towards the palm. We will begin by playing a small *chord* (a chord is two or more notes played together) on the 3rd and 2nd strings. This is an easy place to begin, because it is a lot like making a loose fist. There are three steps—prepare, follow-through, and release:

Step 1. **Prepare** *i* on the 3rd string and *m* on the 2nd string. Let *a* and *c* hang loosely beside *m*. Make sure that your fingers are curled properly. Your knuckle joints should be above the strings you are playing. For instance, since *i* is playing the 3rd string, the *i* knuckle joint should be above the 3rd string. The middle joints should be above the next higher string, so the *i* middle joint should be above the 2nd string. Be sure to place the left edge of your nails and the flesh of your fingertip on the strings together.

Step 2. Gracefully push through the strings towards the back of your palm. Use plenty of knuckle joint movement and even more middle joint movement. Move *a* and *c* too, so that all four fingers move together as a unit. This free-swinging **follow-through** may have to be exaggerated at first, but ultimately, try not to force the fingers in too far. Always try to avoid extremes. The tip joint should be very slightly firm.

Step 3. Let the fingers **release** loosely back to the strings.

There should be a feeling of "controlled letting go." Learning to release your fingers this way is very important to the development of a fluent right-hand technique. The guitar free-stroke release is more controlled than being completely loose because we need to put the fingers back on the strings, but it should feel as much like complete release as possible. As you release, make sure both the knuckle and the middle joints extend together. Never flex one while extending the other.

To keep a steady hand, many students find it helpful to focus on a "fulcrum-point" in the wrist to help brace against the resistance of the strings on the nails and fingers.

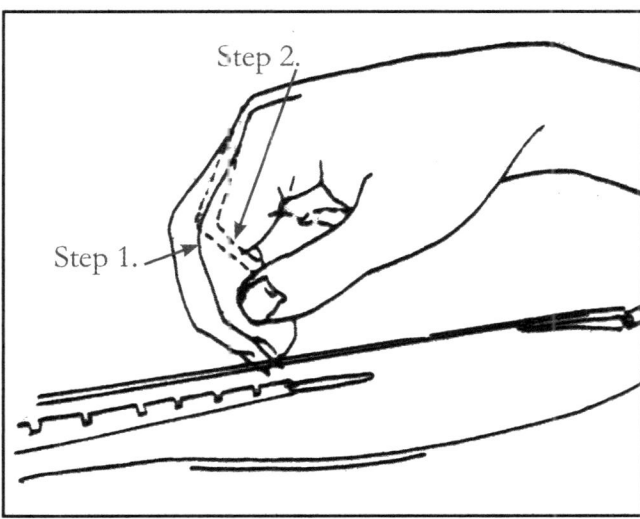
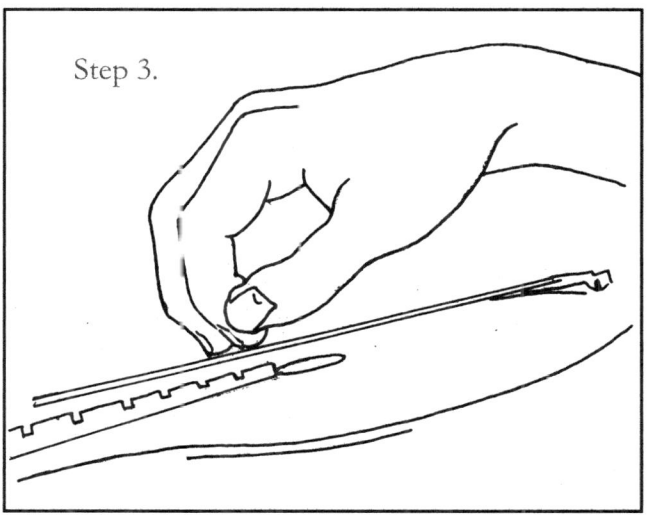

## Introducing Notes on the 3rd, 2nd, and 1st Strings

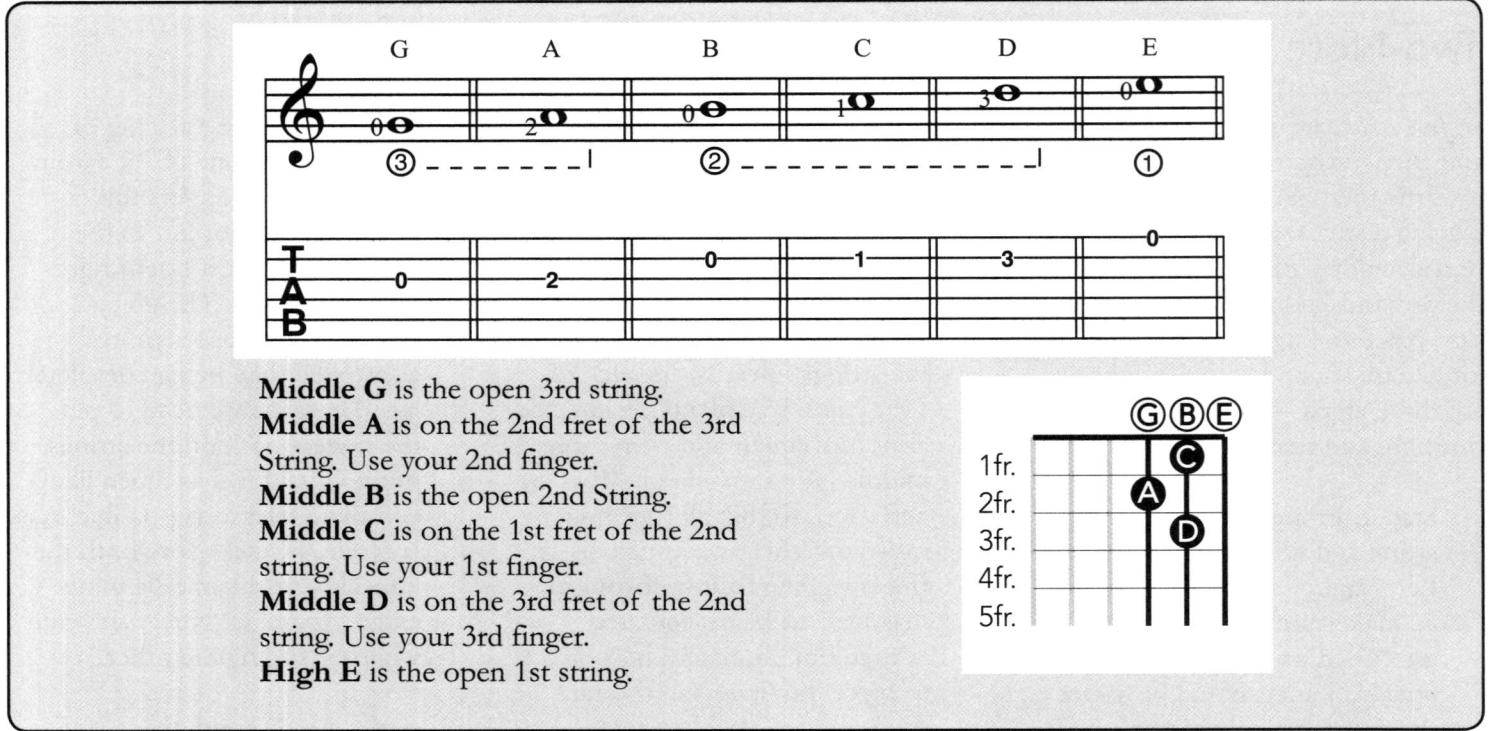

**Middle G** is the open 3rd string.
**Middle A** is on the 2nd fret of the 3rd String. Use your 2nd finger.
**Middle B** is the open 2nd String.
**Middle C** is on the 1st fret of the 2nd string. Use your 1st finger.
**Middle D** is on the 3rd fret of the 2nd string. Use your 3rd finger.
**High E** is the open 1st string.

## Chords on the 3rd and 2nd Strings

Ex.9  Track 22

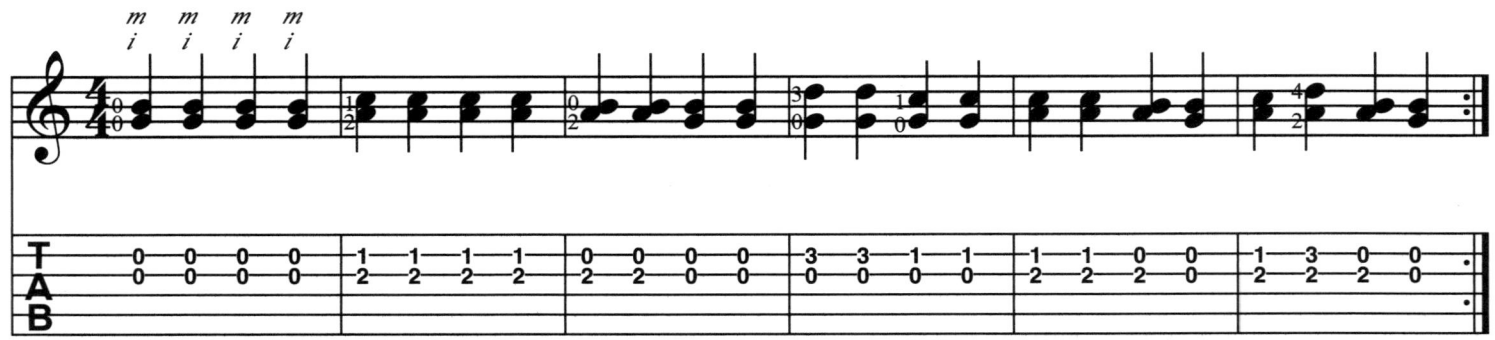

### Tone

There is no substitute for listening to the great artists of our time for learning to distinguish between desirable and undesirable guitar sounds. They may all sound different, but they all have a lot in common. Listen to Andres Segovia, Julian Bream, John Williams, Manuel Barrueco, David Russell, Scott Tennant, the Assads, and other fine players, and you will learn a lot.

In the meantime, your goals should be:
 1. Projection: A firm attack. Good use of the nail. Enough volume so that you can be heard easily from a distance.
 2. Warmth: Good use of the knuckle joint and flesh. A full, dark center to each note.
 3. Edge: Use of the nail and a firm tip joint. A brilliant, crisp attack for each note.
 4. Clarity: Accuracy. Nails in good condition. As little extra-musical noise as possible (clicks, scratches, etc.).

# Crossing Strings

Until now, you have been playing free stroke with *i* and *m* on the 3rd and 2nd strings only. The next exercise has chords on the top two strings: the 2nd and 1st strings. To move your right hand so that *i* and *m* can play on these new strings with exactly the same finger position, move the arm down (towards the top strings and the floor) with your shoulder and elbow joints. You may be able to roll on the flesh of your arm, somewhat, too. Your wrist and hand position should remain unchanged. This is called *crossing*.

It's important to:
1) Continue to stroke the strings in the same location (not further or closer to the bridge); and
2) Keep the position of the hand and fingers constant.

## Chords on the 2nd and 1st Strings

Ex. 10

Pay special attention to the string crossings in this exercise.

Ex. 11

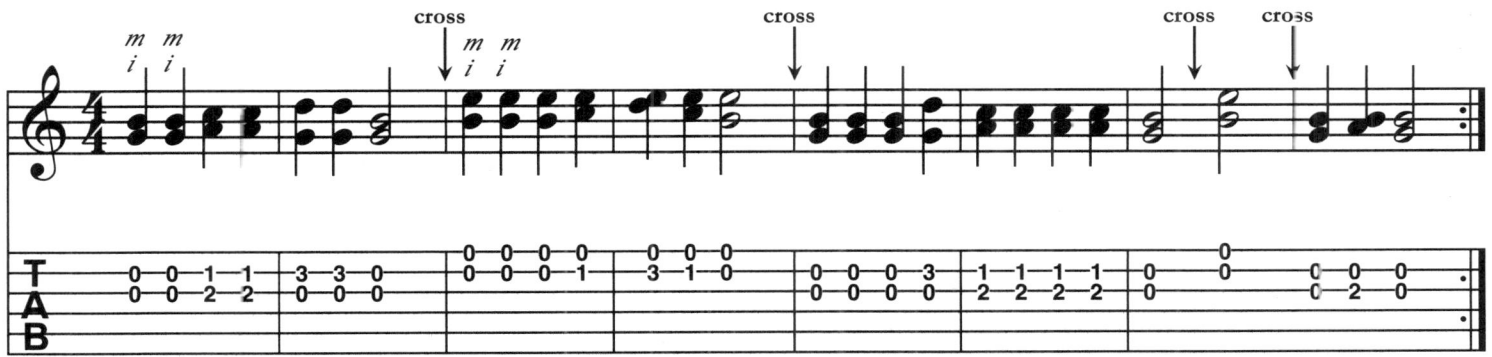

### IMPORTANT

Do the exercises on this page with *m* and *a*, too. The technique is the same, except that *i* will hang loosely beside *m* as *a* and *m* work. Your *c* finger follows *m*.

# Aria (Duet)

Here is another duet to play with a friend, teacher, or the audio for this book. You play the music on the lower staff. Your part should be played entirely with the *p* finger. This Baroque "Aria" was taken from the *Partita in A Minor* for solo lute and arranged as a duet..

by Johann Anton Logy

# INTRODUCING TIES

*Ties* are curved lines connecting two or more successive notes of the same pitch. When two notes are tied, the second one is not picked; its time value is added to the value of the first note. For example:

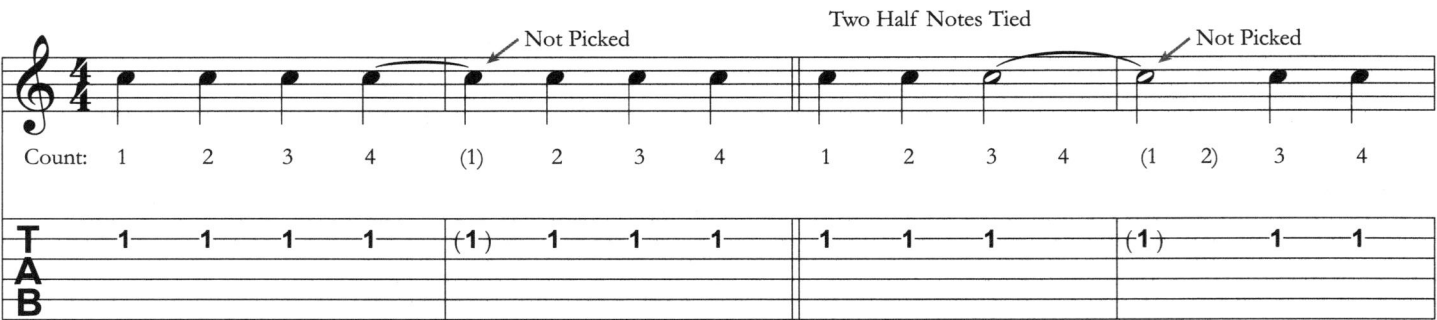

In TAB notation, the tie is indicated by a parenthesis (1)—do not pick that note again.

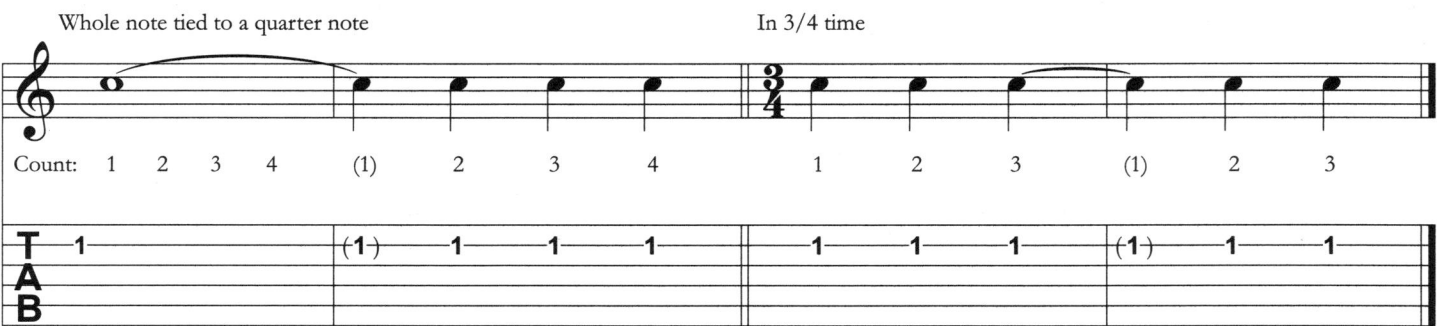

Count aloud as you practice clapping and then playing these rhythms.

**Ex. 12** Track 27

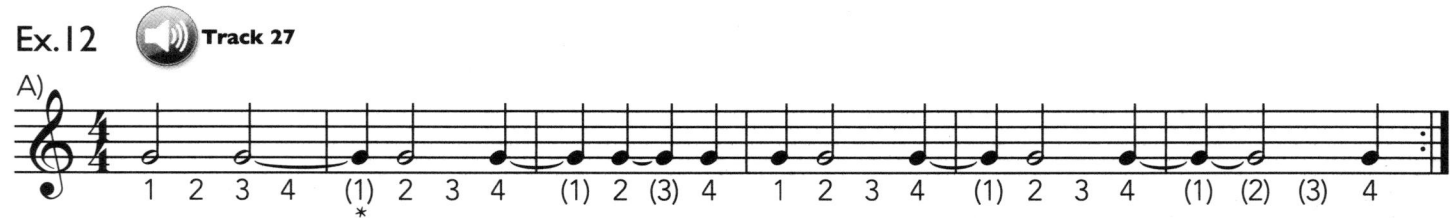

\* Notice that when a note is tied, the counting number is in parentheses.

Track 28

Track 29

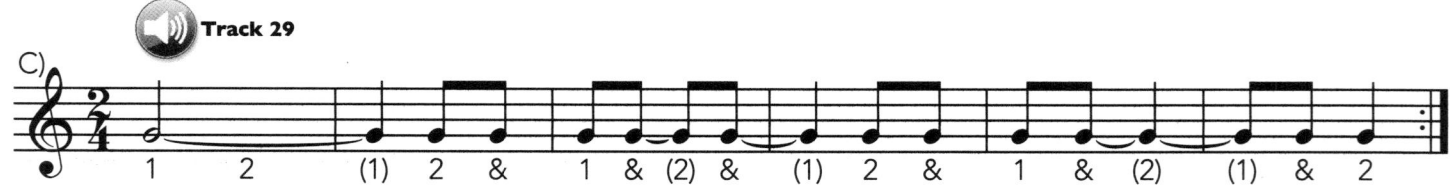

## INTRODUCING DOTTED NOTES

A *dot* increases the length of a note by one half of its original value. For instance, a half note equals two beats. Half of its value is one beat (a quarter note). So a dotted half note is equal to a half note tied to a quarter note.

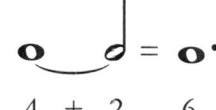

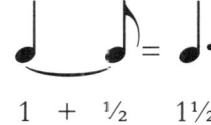

Ex.13

Count aloud as you practice clapping and then playing these rhythms.

A)

**Track 31**

Dotted notes are especially important when the time signature is 3/4 time, because the longest note value that will fit in a measure is a dotted half note.

B)

 **MINI MUSIC LESSON** 6/8 Time

In this time signature, there are six eighth notes in each measure divided into two groups of three, counted "1–&–ah, 2–&–ah."

**Track 32**

Dotted notes are very important in 6/8 time, because not only is a dotted half note the longest possible note value, but a dotted quarter note is exactly half a measure (counted 1 & ah 2 & ah). And, although we can think of there being six eighth notes per measure, we usually count two beats with three eighths in each.

C)

## Introducing High F and G on the 1st String

**High F** is on the 1st fret of the 1st string. Use your 1st finger.
**High G** is on the 3rd fret of the 1st string. Use your 3rd finger.

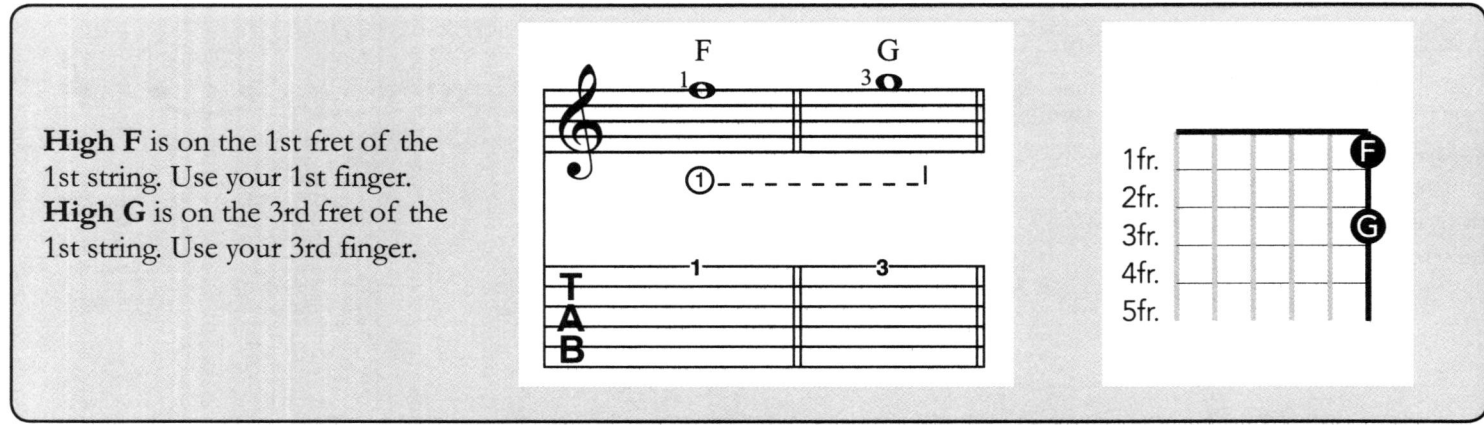

Ex. 14  Track 33

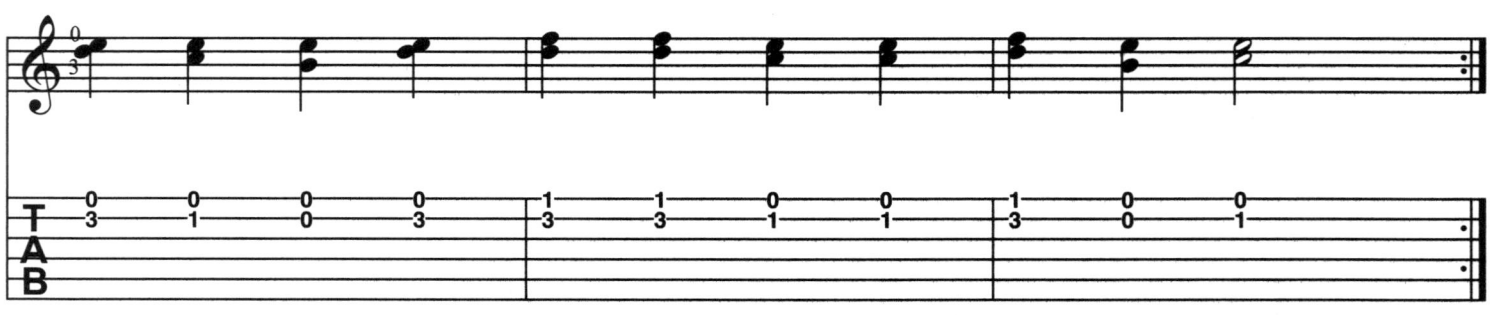

# INTRODUCING ACCIDENTALS (Sharps ♯, Flats ♭, and Naturals ♮)

An *accidental* is a symbol that alters the pitch of a note.

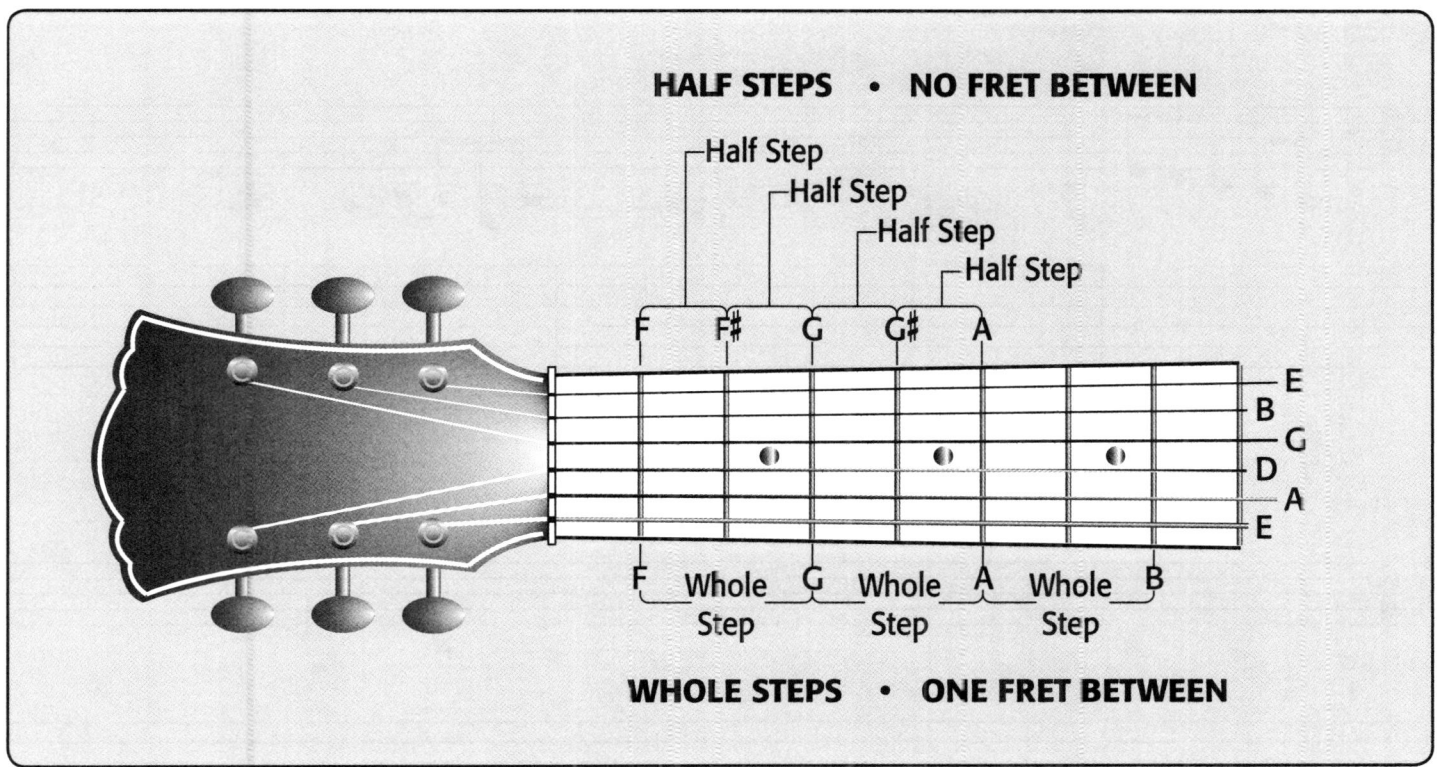

 ## Accidental Signs

♯   SHARPS **raise** the note a half step. Play the next fret higher.

♭   FLATS **lower** the note a half step. If the note is fingered, play the next fret lower. If the note is open, play the 4th fret of the next lower string—except if that string is **G** (3rd string), then play the 3rd fret.

♮   NATURALS **cancel** a previous sharp or flat.

When added within a measure, sharps, flats, and naturals are called *accidentals*.
A bar line cancels a previous accidental in the measures that follow.

# 32 TEACH YOURSELF TO PLAY CLASSICAL GUITAR

Here are three tunes with accidentals to play.

# ALTERNATING BETWEEN THUMB AND FINGERS USING FREE STROKES

If you have learned to hold your hand steady during thumb strokes without resting fingers on the strings, and feel comfortable with two-note chords, it's time to combine the two techniques into one technique called an *alternation*. This is the natural next step, and you will find it a fairly easy one.

Start by combining *i–m* chords with *p*. Begin by placing *i* and *m* on the 3rd and 2nd strings respectively. Complete a free-stroke, and then hold your fingers inside your palm. Now prepare *p* on your 5th string and you are ready to go.

1. Digging-in with the tip of *p*, play the 5th string while simultaneously releasing *i* and *m* to their strings. You should end up with the very end of the pad of *p* resting against the tip of *i*.
2. As you push through the 3rd and 2nd strings with *i* and *m*, extend *p* back to the 5th string.

The arrows in Example 15 illustrate the alternation between *p* and the fingers.

Ex. 15    Track 37

Notice that this music is written in two parts. The treble part (being played by *i* and *m*) rests on the first two beats of the first measure, while the bass (being played by *p*) plays an A whole note, and later, half notes.

As the exercise proceeds, the treble part is written stems up, and the bass part is written stems down. Two-part writing such as this, and even three- and four-part writing, is common in the classical guitar repertoire.

Try the same thing using *m* and *a* on the 2nd and 1st strings with *p* on the 5th string.

### IMPORTANT: Technical Check

Remember to hold your hand steady. Also, it is important to note that when you combine finger movements of any kind in an alternation, they become a bit trickier to do. Make sure the quality of both the thumb and finger strokes is the same in this alternation as they are separately. For instance, do a few individual *p* strokes before trying this alternation. Check to make sure your tip and wrist are extending together, that your tip is slightly flexed as you prepare on the string, and that your follow-through is direct and free all the way to *i*. There should be no circular movements either extending or following-through. Now try the alternation as described above. The thumb movement should be identical to the solo strokes you just did. Do the same sort of check with *i* and *m*.

Combining the thumb and fingers this way opens up a lot of possibilities for music making on the guitar. The following exercises and pieces will be very satisfying for you if you practice slowly and carefully. Enjoy!

# PIECES WITH THUMB AND TWO-NOTE CHORD ALTERNATIONS

Remember to prepare, repeat, and review! Play very slowly, practicing very small portions at first, and you will be sounding great soon. Master each piece before going on to the next.

## Country Dance No. 1 — Track 38

## Homage to Villa-Lobos — Track 39

# In the Style of Leo Brouwer

 Track 40

Learn just the bass part to this one, first. When added to the treble part, what looks like a complicated rhythm sounds like continuous eighth notes!

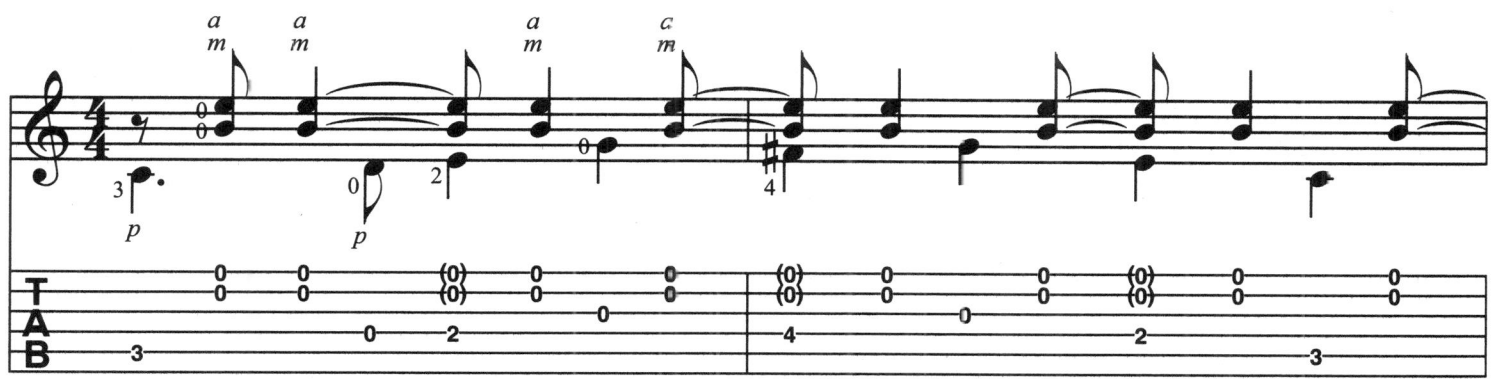

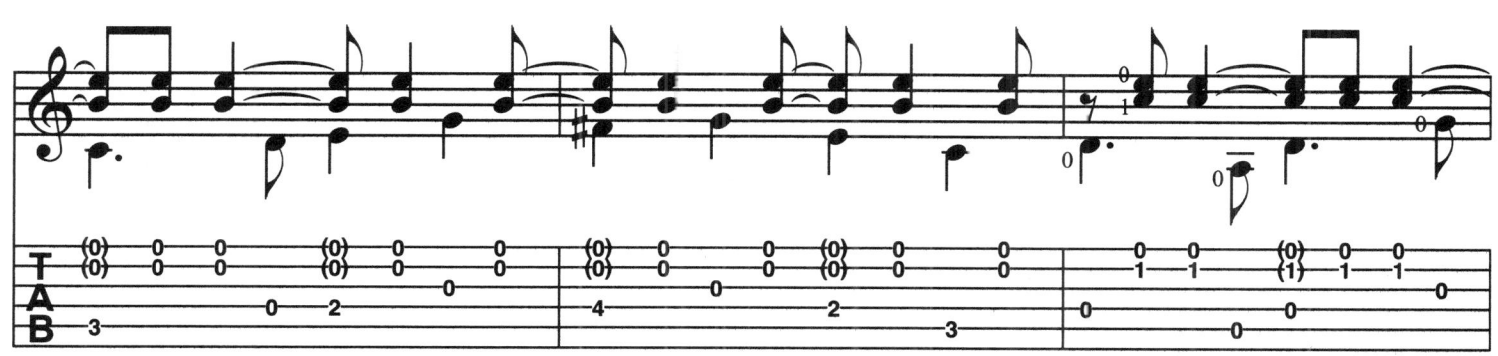

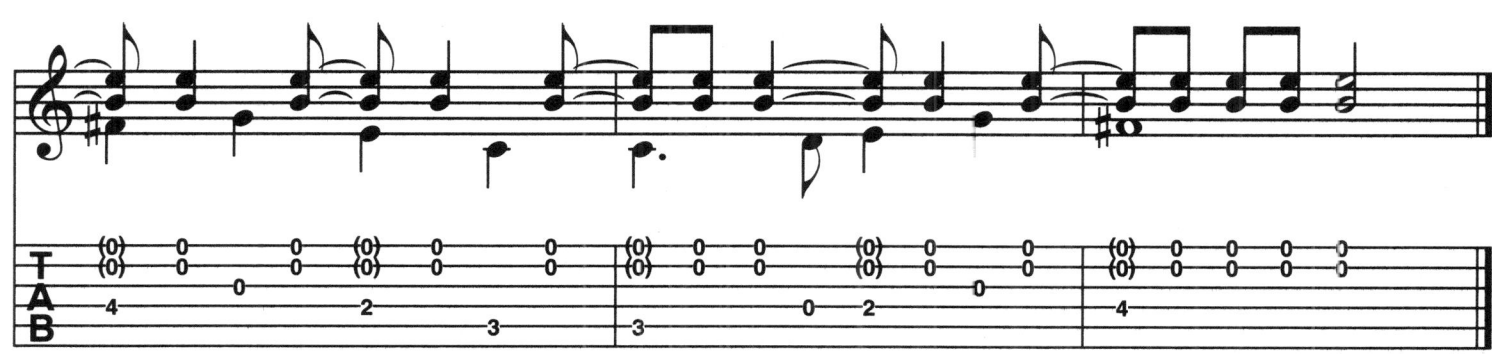

# INCOMPLETE MEASURES AND PICKUP NOTES

Not every piece of music begins on beat 1. Sometimes, music begins with an incomplete measure called an *upbeat*, or *pickup*. If the pickup has just one beat, the last measure will have only three beats in 4/4 or two beats in 3/4.

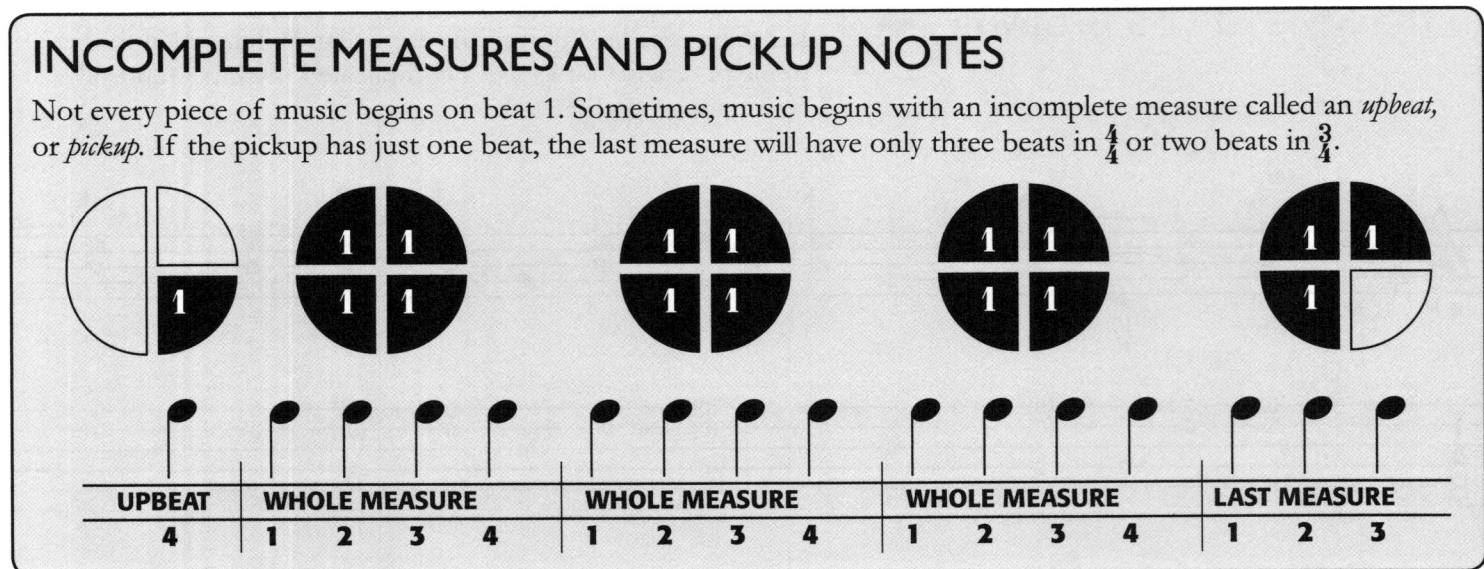

## Grazioso (Duet)

Track 41 Both Parts   Track 42 Accompaniment

Here's a duet for you to enjoy playing with a friend, teacher, or the audio for this book. You play the lower staff.

Notice that this piece starts with a *pickup note*, or *anacrusis*. A pickup note is one that occurs before the first complete measure. In this case, the pickup note is one eighth note. The last measure of the piece is one eighth note short of being a complete measure, thus accounting for the extra eighth note at the beginning.

by Mauro Giuliani

*Excerpt from*
## Terpsichore (Duet)

Here's another, just for fun!

by José Ferrer

# SHIFTING UP THE NECK

So far, all the notes you have learned are in *open position*. In other words, the pieces have used notes on the open strings and the first four frets of the guitar. This is a great way to get started. But what about the rest of the frets? The addition of *shifting* to your left-hand technique will give you access to all those other frets. This makes the fingerboard of the guitar a very rich and exciting place.

A *shift* is a change in position. In other words, if you move your left hand up the neck (to the right) out of open position to a higher one, you have shifted. Try Example 16. Play the low F with your 1st finger. Then, during the rest, release the pressure on the F and, keeping the 1st finger very lightly touching the string, slowly slide it up to the G on the 3rd fret. Play the G with the 1st finger. Congratulations! You have shifted to 3rd position. This kind of shift is called a *guide finger* shift.

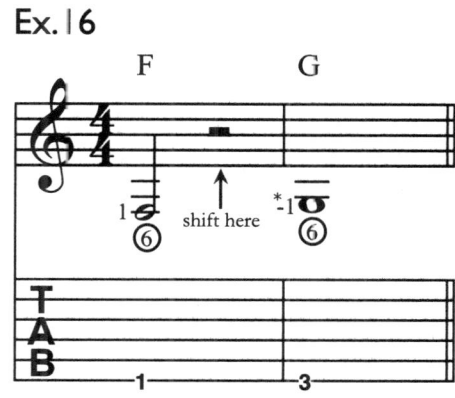

Ex. 16

* A dash (-) before a fingering shows that you have shifted.

> **Fret Markers**
>
> If your guitar does not have fret markers on the side of the neck (dots), you can add some of your own to help find the notes in the upper positions. Put white non-residue tape at the 5th, 7th, 10th, and 12th frets. Eventually, you'll want to remove these because classical guitars do not typically have position markers. You will soon be able to find your way around without them.

> **Positions**
>
> The name of each position comes from the fret number your 1st finger is on. 5th position is when your 1st finger is on the 5th fret.

On page 5 of this book, you learned how to tune the 5th string of the guitar by comparing it to the 5th fret of the 6th string. This works because the 5th fret of the 6th string is a low A, just the same as the open 5th string. So, using shifting technique, you could choose to play low A on the 6th string instead of the 5th if the context makes it a good choice. You can also play low B and low C on the 6th string.

## 40 TEACH YOURSELF TO PLAY CLASSICAL GUITAR

Ex. 17  Track 45

In Example 17A below, you will first play the notes E–F–G–A–B–C in the familiar open position. In Example 17B, you will play the very same notes, but remain on the 6th string for all of them! You will play A, C, and E in *5th position* (with your 1st finger on the 5th fret). Pay close attention to the string numbers (circled), left-hand fingerings (not circled), and fret numbers (5fr. is the 5th fret, 7fr. is the 7th fret, etc.). Shift very slowly and lightly during the rests.

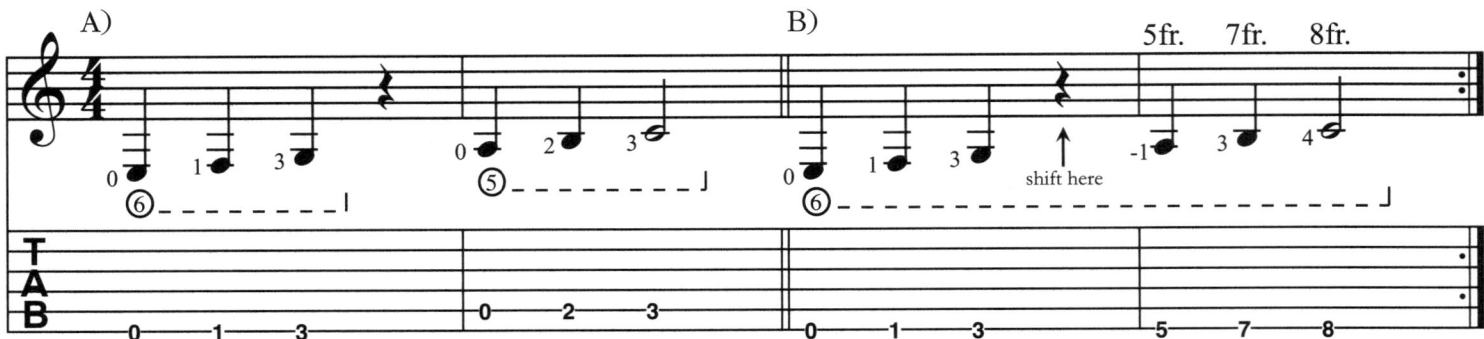

Ex. 18  Track 46

Take this idea one step further and add another shift up to low D and middle E on the 6th string. You will be playing D, E, and F in *10th position* (with your 1st finger on the 10th fret). Shift slowly and lightly.

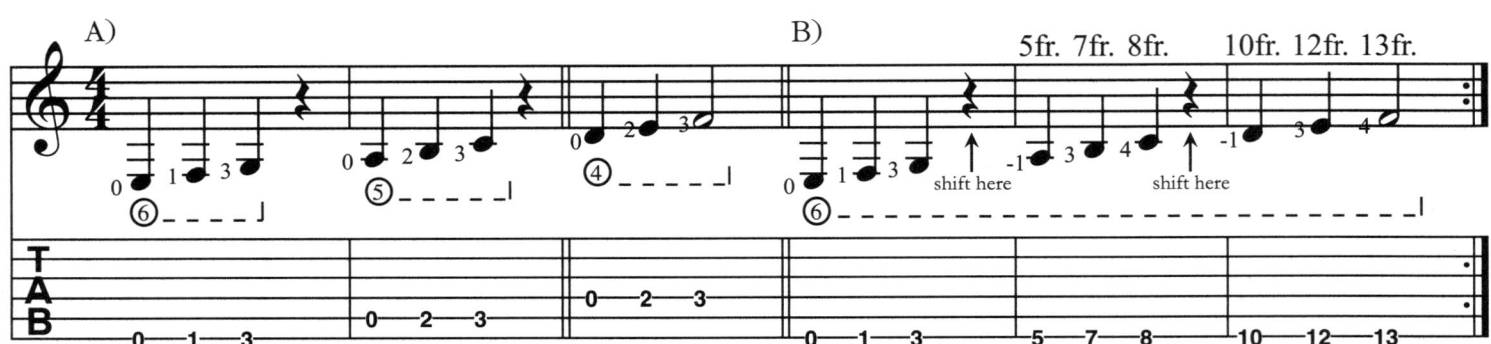

Ex. 19  Track 47

Now, use shifting to play in the higher positions of the 5th string. Remember to shift as slowly as possible during the rests, just barely touching the string as you move.

Example 19 uses one shift to play low D, middle E, and F on the 5th string.

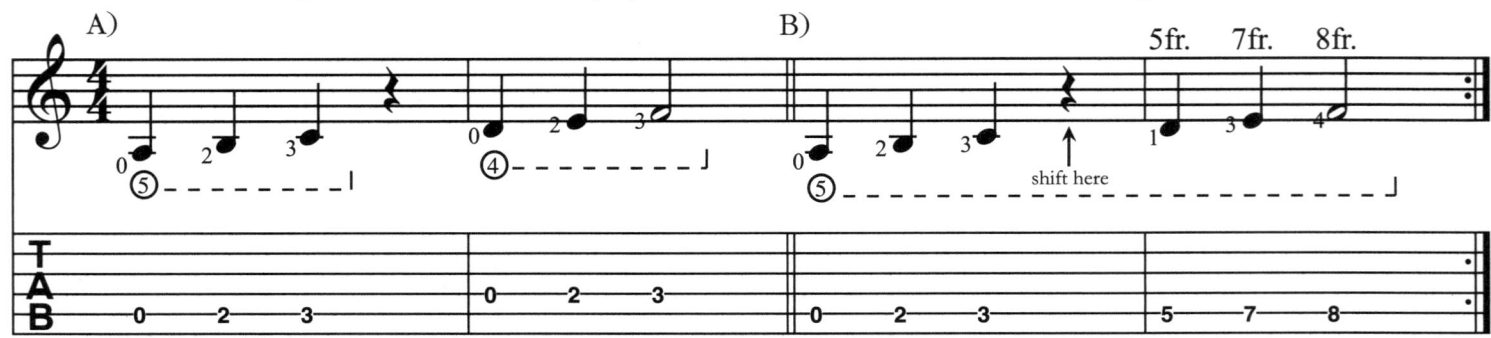

Ex.20  **Track 48**

Example 20 uses two shifts to include middle G and A, as well.

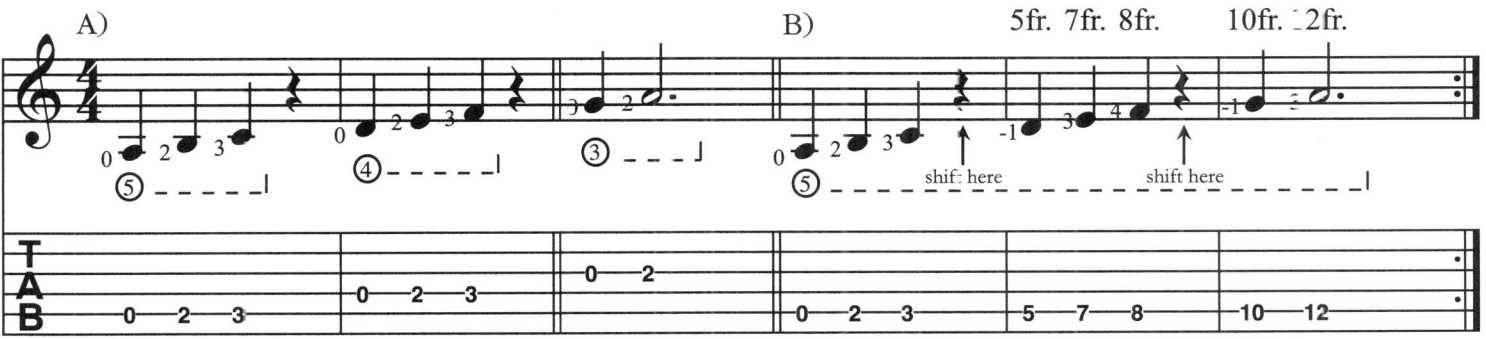

Don't rush through these exercises. It is very important to attain a thorough knowledge of the guitar fingerboard, and there is no time like the present. If you take your time and shift slowly during the rests, you will find shifting easy. As you become more advanced you will learn to shift in less than a heartbeat, moving up and down the fingerboard with ease and grace.

To eventually attain that ease and grace, however, you need to keep things easy, for now. You can never learn ease by practicing difficulty! So, concentrate, play slowly, shift slowly, and lightly.

It is very important to notice the different sound that results from playing a note in a higher position. For instance, low B played on the 6th string sounds much warmer—fatter—than the same note played on the 5th string. Musicians use the word *timbre* (pronounced TAM-bur) to discuss the quality of sound. The low B on the 6th string has a different timbre than the low B on the 5th string. Often, the desire for a particular timbre will govern our choices about where to finger notes.

### Ferdinando Carulli

*Born in Italy in 1770, Ferdinando Carulli died in Paris in 1841. He wrote a comprehensive guitar method (Opus 241) in 1810 and a book on the art of accompaniment, "L'Harmonique Applique A La Guitarre" in 1825. Carulli composed more than 400 works for guitar, including many student pieces and chamber works.*

Here are some studies that involve shifting to upper positions on the lower strings.

## Spanish Romance  Track 49

"Spanish Romance" is a favorite among classical guitarists and audiences. It will sound very beautiful played slowly and expressively mostly on the 5th string. There are several different kinds of shifts in this melody. At [A], play the D on the open 4th string while you shift your left hand down to open position. At [B], keep your 1st finger lightly on the string as you move swiftly and gracefully from the 3rd to the 7th frets. This is a guide finger shift. At [C], shift your hand down to substitute your 4th finger for your 1st finger. As usual, practice carefully: prepare, repeat, and review. It is also important to isolate and practice each shift—the notes before, beneath, and just after each arrow.

↓ = shift here

Traditional

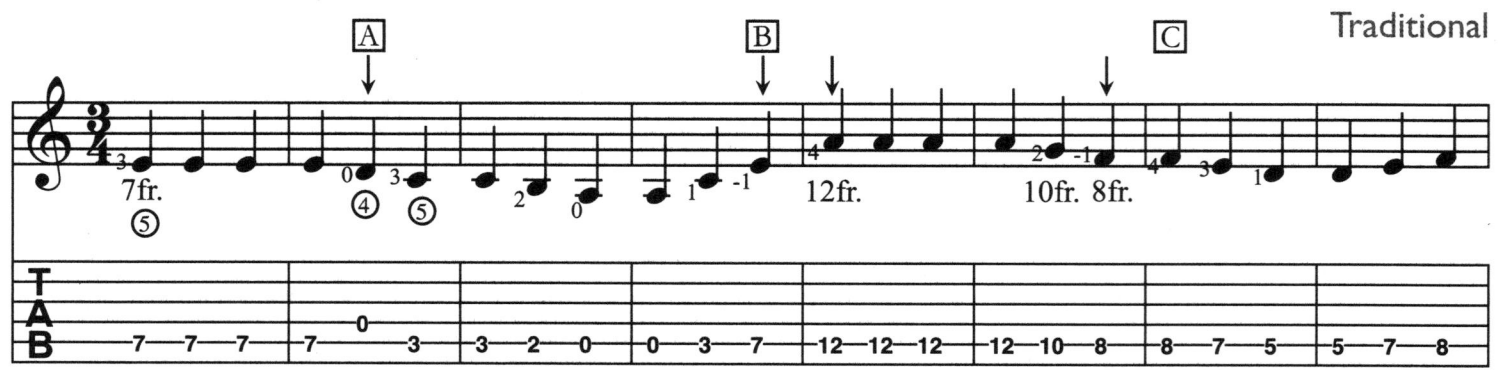

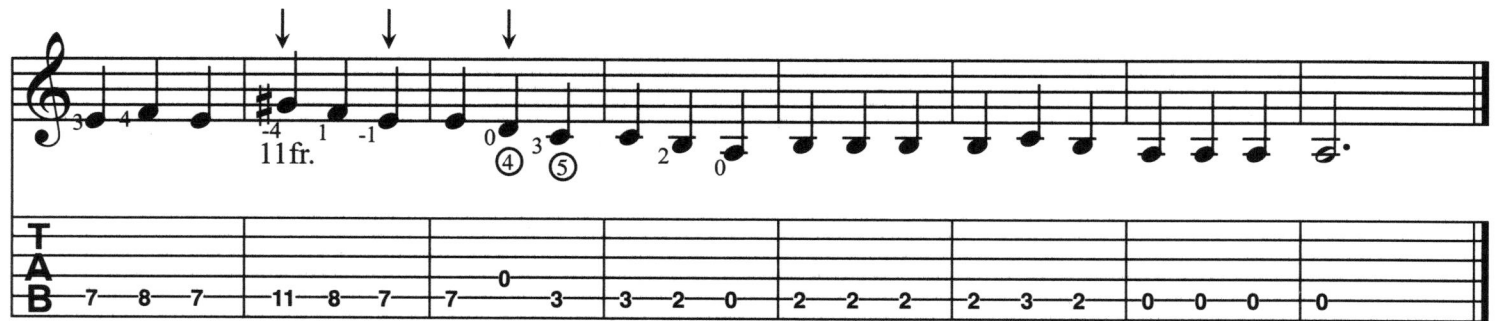

## Theme from FUGA, BWV 1000  Track 50

Here is another famous melody from our repertoire. There are two versions of this piece one for violin and another for lute.

by Johann Sebastian Bach

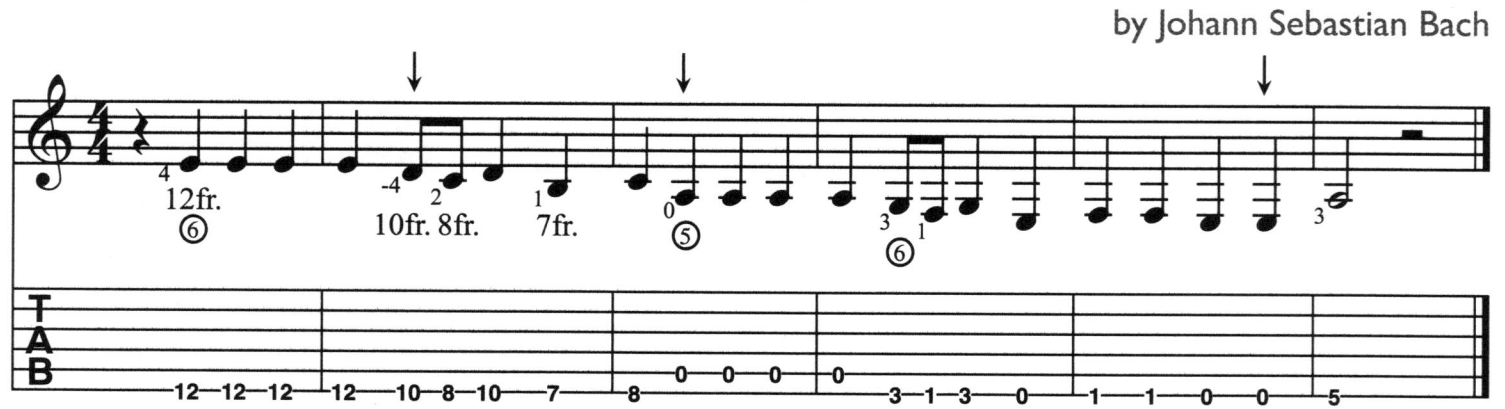

## ALTERNATING p WITH INDIVIDUAL FINGER STROKES

Ex. 21  Track 51

By now, you are becoming comfortable with two-note, free-stroke chords. In Example 21, you will play single notes with *i*, *m*, and *a*. The finger movements are the same as for two-note chords except that each finger plays alone. Remember that when *m* plays, *a* and *c* should move with it while *i* hangs loosely. When *a* plays, *c* should move with it while *i* and *m* hang loosely.

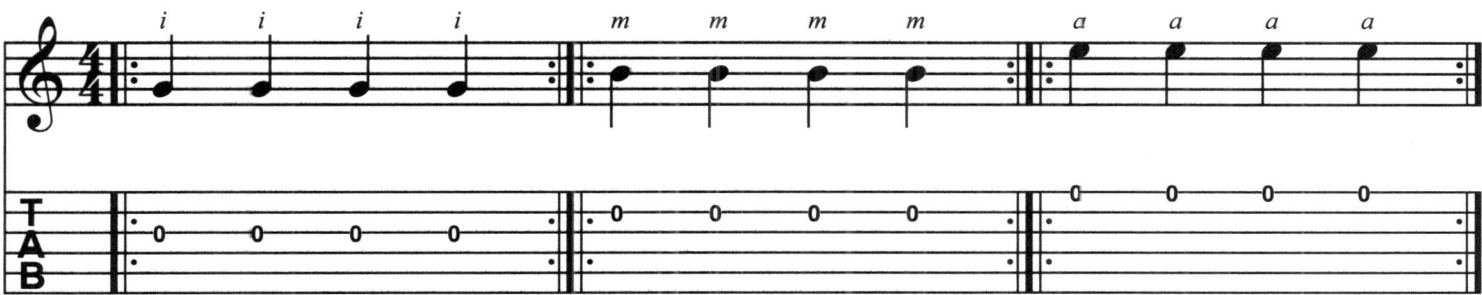

Alternating *p* with individual finger strokes is very much like *p* alternating with two-note chords. The only difference is that the fingers are working more independently. The musical options that result are very rich.

Ex. 22  Track 52

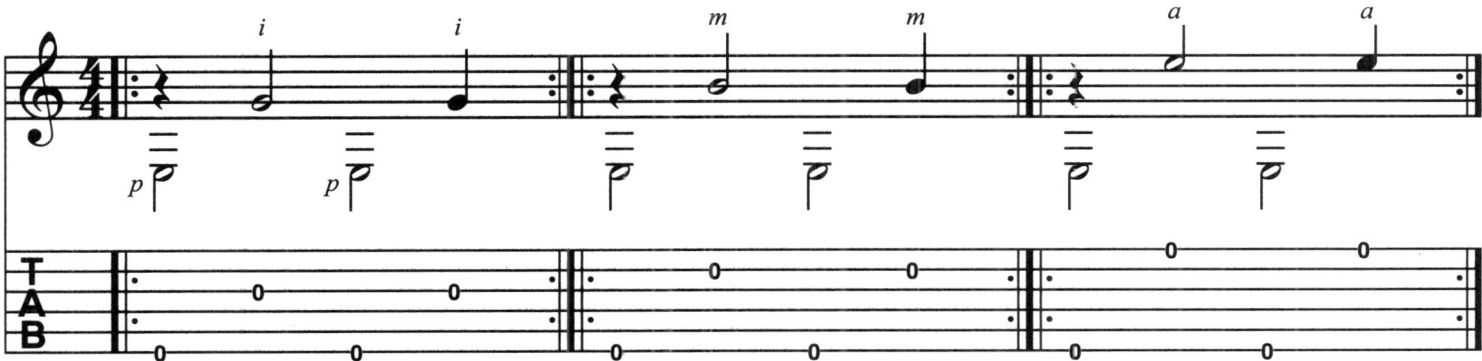

Ex.23  

Ex.24

Ex.25

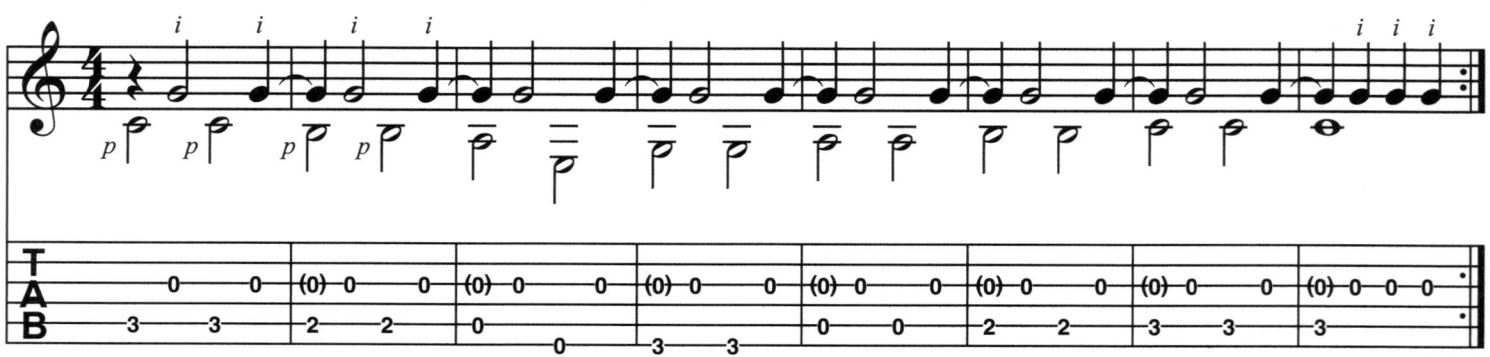

# TEACH YOURSELF TO PLAY CLASSICAL GUITAR 45

## *Theme from* Asturias (Leyenda)  Track 56

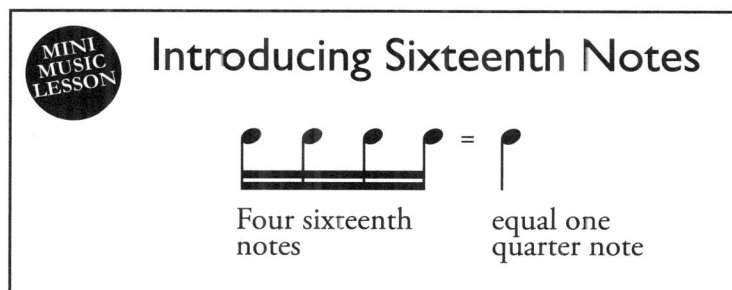

"Leyenda" is perhaps the most famous classical guitar piece, although it was originally composed for the piano.

You will notice that each eighth note in this piece has two stems, one going up (sixteenth notes) and one going down (eighth notes). This is a convenient way to show two things:
1. The continuous sixteenth-note rhythm; and
2. The bass notes and treble notes have the distinctively different roles of melody (bass) and accompaniment (treble).

Use *m* on the open B string and *p* in the bass throughout.

by Isaac Albéniz

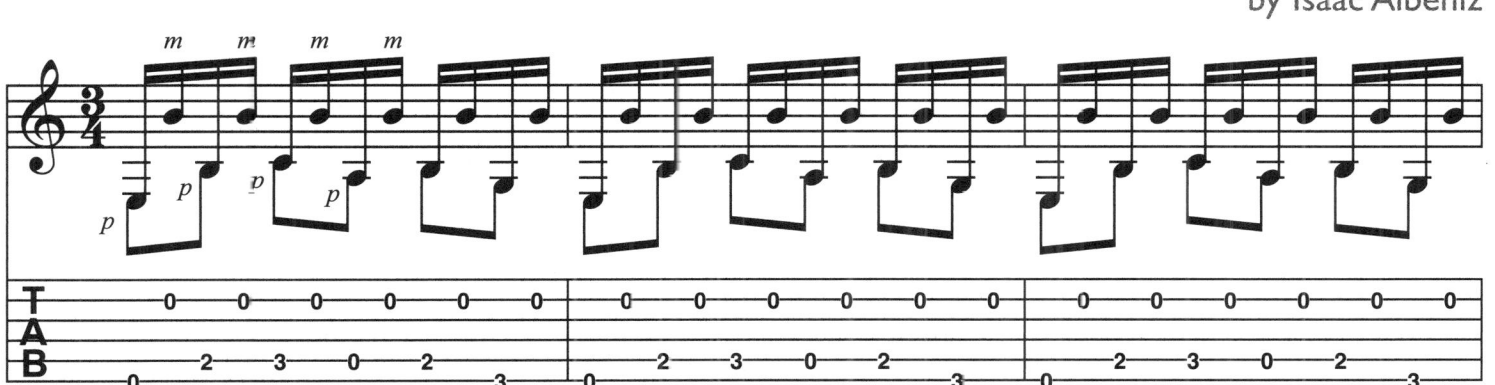

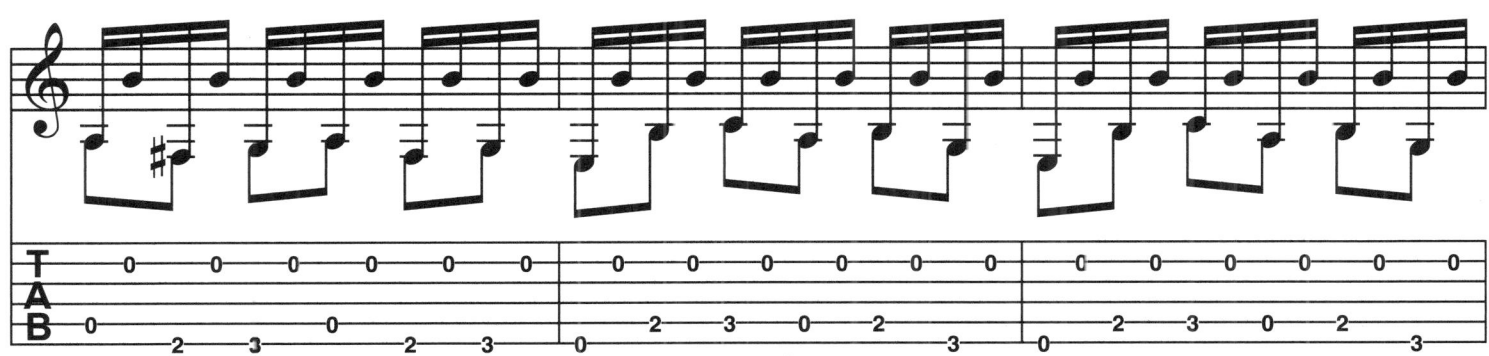

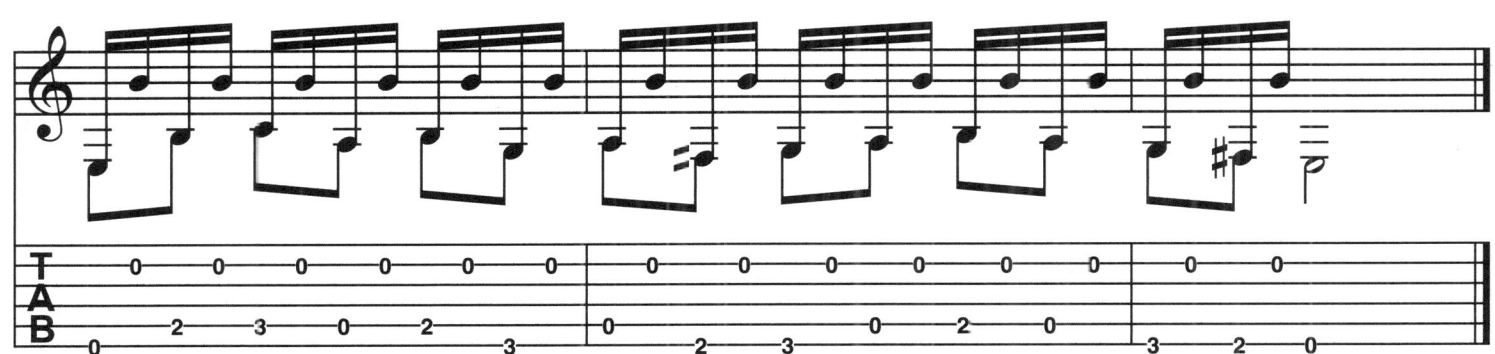

## Theme from Malagueña

If "Leyenda" isn't the most famous guitar piece, then "Malagueña" surely is. It's really a flamenco piece, but when people find out that you play the classical guitar, you'll be asked to play it. This excerpt will get you started. Hold down all the notes with the left hand for as long as you can, letting the notes ring through one another.

Traditional Flamenco Melody

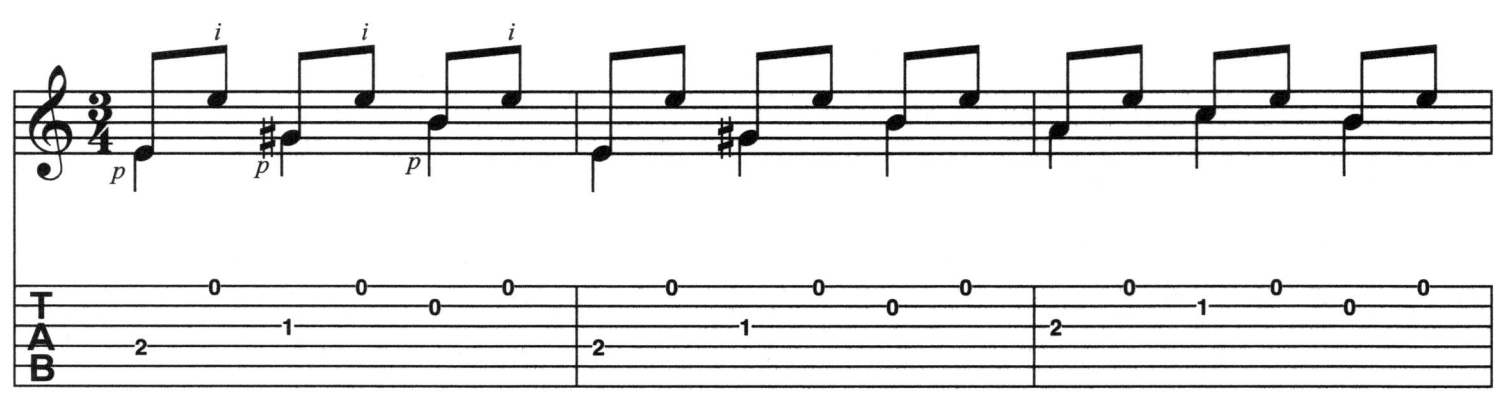
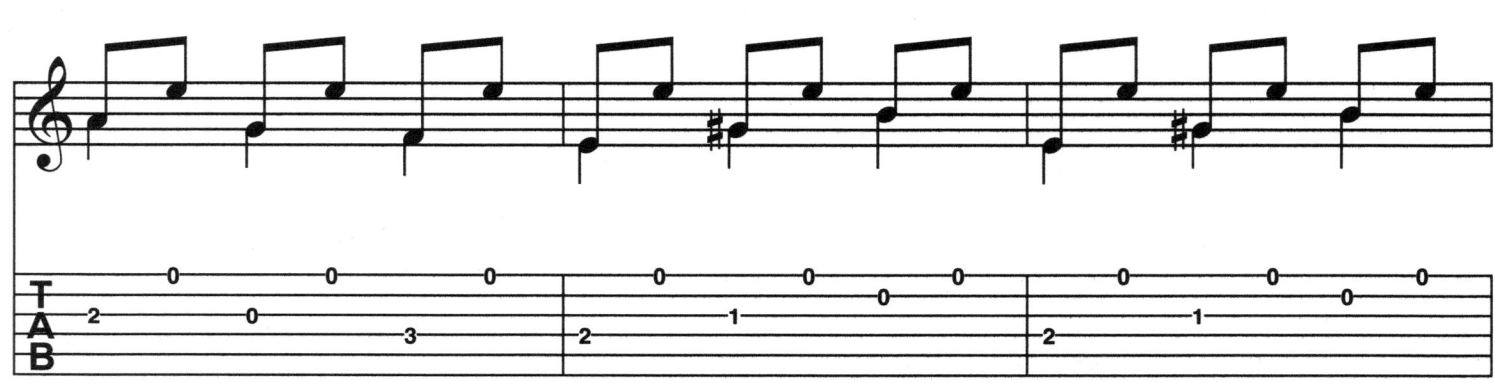
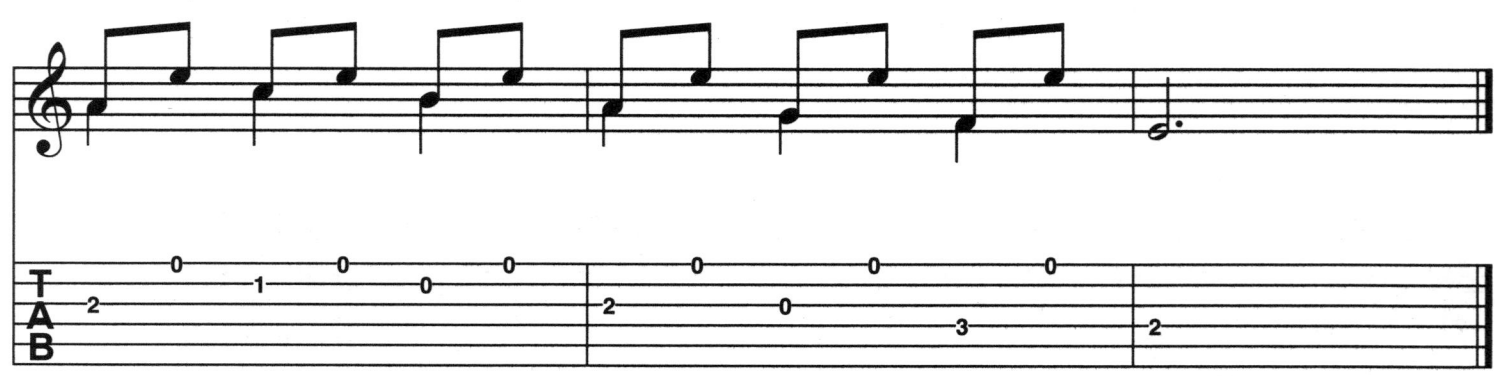

# INTRODUCING REST STROKE (APOYANDO)

*Rest stroke* is a very important right-hand technique. Because it relies a bit more on the knuckle joint than the free stroke, it can be somewhat stronger sounding. While a good free stroke can be about as strong and rich sounding as a rest stroke, it is easier to achieve a big sound with rest stroke. Also, since it does not involve a follow-through, you may one day find it more useful for rapid scales.

> We will use these symbols to mark rest stroke and free stroke:
>
> ▽ = Rest stroke
> ∪ = Free stroke

## The Position

Put your *i* finger in position for free stroke on the 3rd string. Your knuckle joint should float above the 3rd string and your middle joint above the 2nd. Now, without crossing from the elbow or moving the hand in any way, reach *i* out to the 1st string. Your knuckle joint should still be above the 3rd string and your middle above the 2nd—but now the nail and flesh of the finger are prepared on the 1st string. This results in a slightly more extended, less curled, finger position.

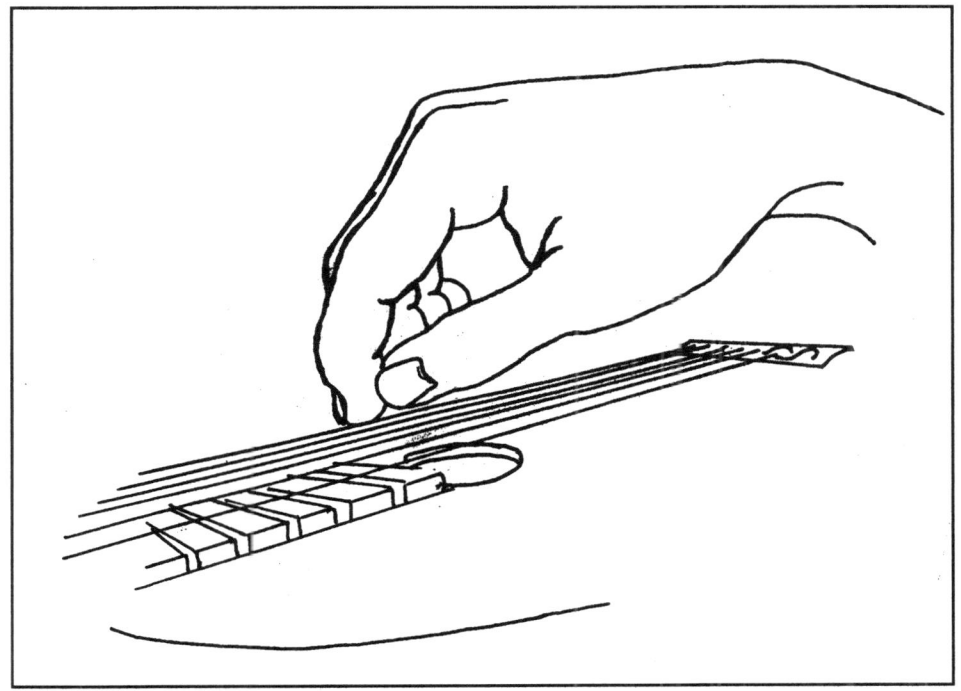

*The right-hand position for rest stroke.*

### Augustiín Barrios-Mangoré

*Barrios's (1885–1944) performances were compared to Segovia for their interpretation and to Paganini for their virtuosity. He composed over 100 works. Some of his pieces are now in the standard repertoire. Barrios was the first classical guitarist to make a gramophone recording.*

## The Stroke

As with every stroke you have learned so far, there are three steps to playing a rest stroke.

Prepare *i* on the string using the method described on page 47. Check your position carefully and try this on the 1st string.

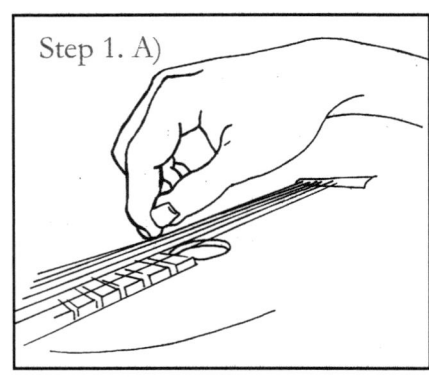

Step 1. A) Keeping your tip joint firm, but not tight, push down on the string with the knuckle joint while pulling sharply across from the middle. B) You should land on the next string over, (hence the name rest stroke) on the very end of your finger. If you did not pull adequately from the middle joint, you will be resting too far down on the tip segment of your finger, almost under the string you played, which would make the next step difficult, requiring an awkward circular movement to extend.

Step 2. If you are resting far enough on the end of your finger, this step will be a breeze. Lift your finger up and away from the guitar using the knuckle almost exclusively. The middle joint should release, but not extend. Lift the finger up high from the knuckle, but at this point your middle joint should be no more extended or flexed than it would be if your finger were prepared on the string.

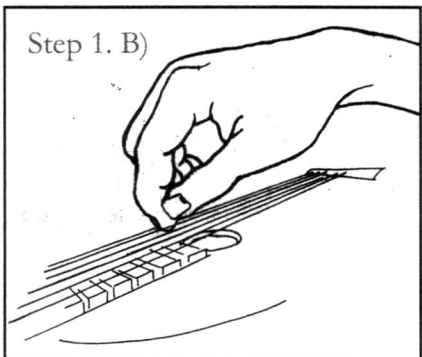

Step 3. Let the finger drop loosely, with a feeling of release, back to the 1st string. If your hand has remained steady and you released the middle joint properly in Step 2, and didn't overextend it, it should feel as though the string is right where you left it! Voila! You should be back where you started. Again, be careful to make sure there are no circular, pedaling type movements.

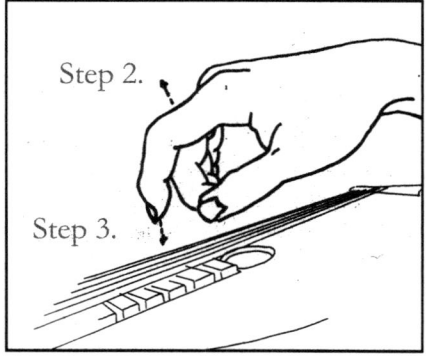

 **IMPORTANT**

A very common error students make when learning this stroke is, during Step 2, to flex the middle joint while extending the knuckle. This is quite unnecessary and involves extra work. Fingers moving this way have the appearance of pedaling, as your legs do when riding a bike. Try pedaling your *i* finger in the air in front of you. Now try an in and out (or up and down) movement where both joints move together. You will sense how much less energy is required for this non-pedaling movement, right away.

Try rest stroke with *m* and *a*, too. You will have to adjust your arm position upwards a bit to put *m* in rest-stroke position on the 1st string, and then up a bit more for *a*. Repeat each finger many times, until you feel confident with the stroke. Do this repeatedly until confident before trying the next section.

# Rest Stroke Alternation

Alternating *i* and *m* in rest stroke is probably one of the most frequently used right-hand techniques. We tend to play most melodies this way.

Adjusting as necessary from the elbow joint, position *i* in rest-stroke position on the 3rd string and *m* in rest-stroke position on the 2nd string. The *i* middle joint should be above the 4th string, and the knuckle above the 5th, while the *m* middle joint should be above the 3rd string, and the knuckle above the 4th.

Now, without playing, lift the *m* knuckle joint up and poise it to play—do not change the middle joint position at all! Keeping *m* poised to play, play the 3rd string with *i*, getting into a resting position with the very end of the finger resting on the 4th string. You are now ready to start alternating.

### Alternate!

Very, very slowly and mechanically (for now), begin to move *m* down towards the 2nd string as you simultaneously begin to lift *i* up off of the 4th. Remember to avoid any circular, pedaling style movements. This should look like it's being done in slow motion. When *m* finally reaches the 2nd string—don't stop for long—play the string and keep *i* moving out to a poised position. Congratulations, you have completed one full alternation! Now, just reverse things and bring *i* down as *m* lifts up. Try this exact same process with *m* and *a*, on the 2nd and 1st strings.

Ex.26

> **MINI GUITAR LESSON**
>
> **IMPORTANT**
>
> The two most important things to remember are these: the fingers should move in opposite directions at exactly the same time and there should be no awkward, circular, pedaling-style movements. Practicing this way—very slowly and carefully—you will become confident with rest stroke alternation in a short time.

Ex.27  **Track 59**

Now let's try alternating on one string. The technique is exactly the same, but, since you will be playing with both fingers on the 2nd string, you will need to adjust your arm position down (towards the floor) ever so slightly, so that both fingers are as close to their ideal rest-stroke positions as possible. Now, repeat the **Alternate!** section on page 49 with both fingers playing the 2nd string.

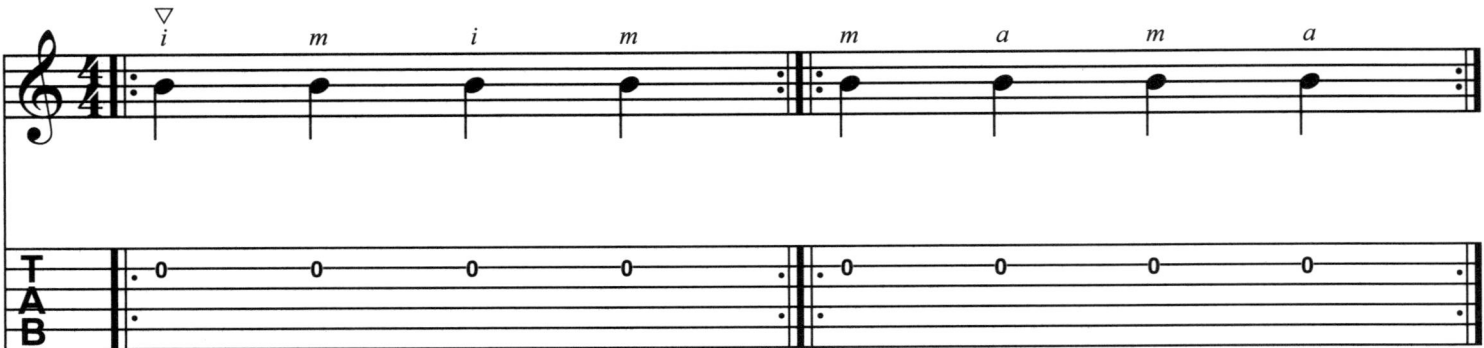

Ex.28  **Track 60**

Now, try crossing from the 2nd string to the 1st and back again. Remember, this is done by moving the arm. The finger and hand positions remain constant, no matter which string you are on.

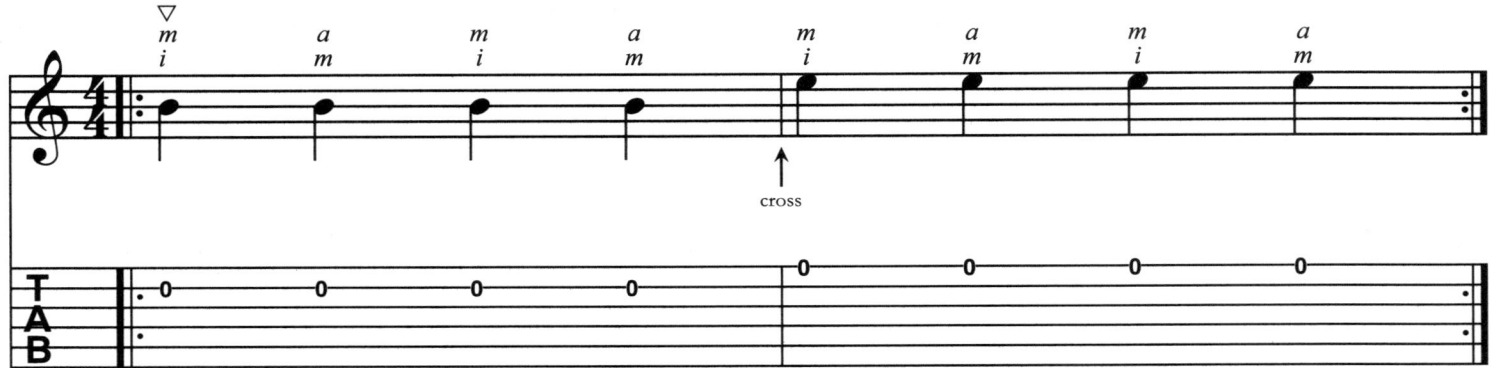

## Dionisio Aguado

*Aguado was born in Madrid, Spain in 1784, and died there in 1849. He was an important exponent of the use of the right-hand fingernails, in contrast to his friend Fernando Sor, who played on his flesh. While he was not as prolific as Sor, his works show great depth. Aguado was also the inventor of a device called the tripodison (pictured in his portrait on the right), which was a three-legged stand designed to help guitarists support the instrument. Unlike his wonderful compositions, the tripodison did not endure.*

# TEACH YOURSELF TO PLAY CLASSICAL GUITAR 51

## Alternating *p* with Rest Strokes

To alternate *p* and *i* rest stroke, simply begin to extend *p* every time *i* begins to drop down to the string, and extend *i* every time *p* plays.

Remember to check that the quality of each stroke, for both *p* and *i*, is the same during this alternation as in individual strokes. Go back and read about comparing non-alternating strokes to alternations in the Technical Check section on page 33.

Ex.29 Track 61

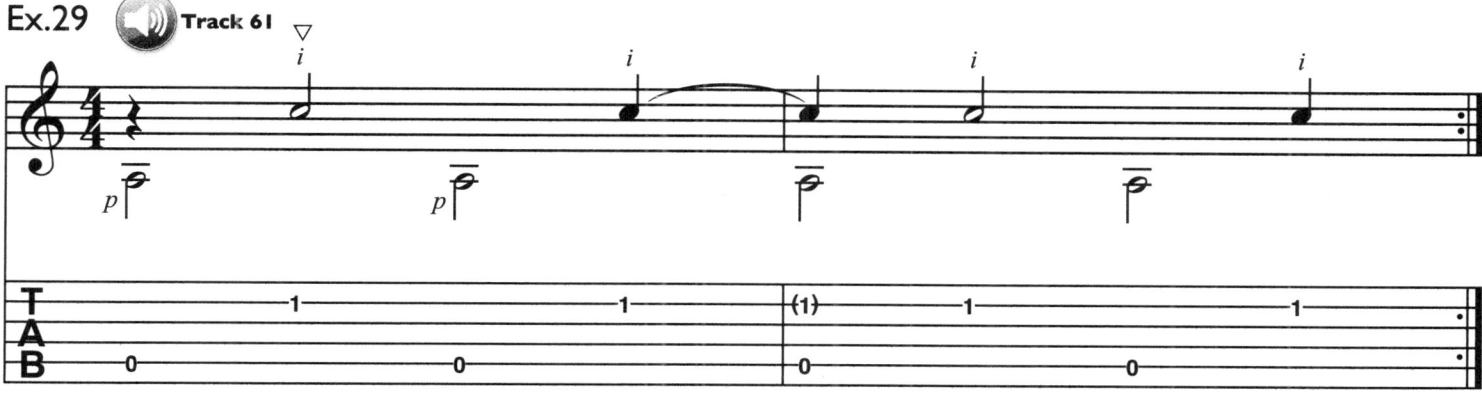

Ex.30 Track 62

Try the same technique using *m* and then *a*.

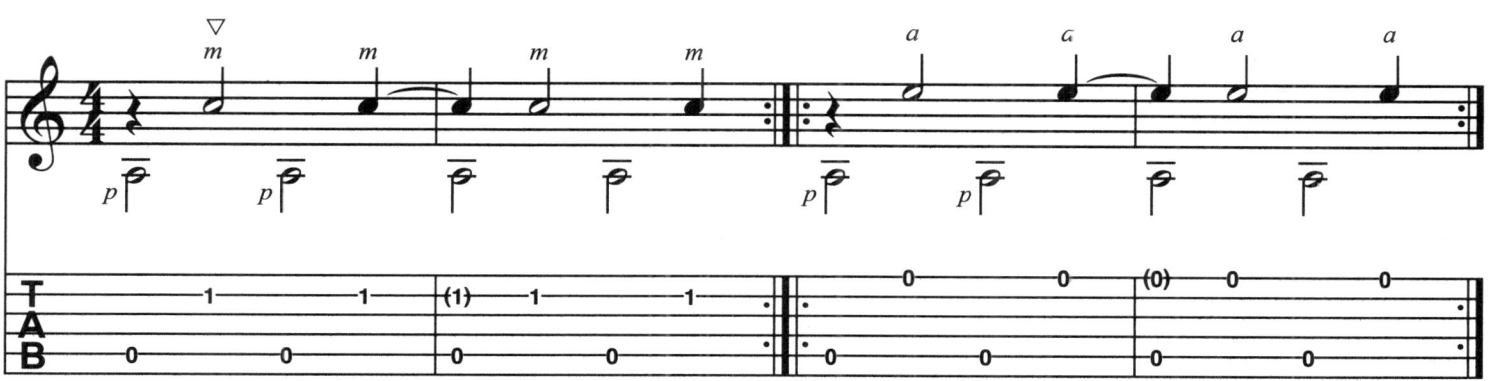

Ex.31 Track 63

Be sure to learn Example 31 with both of the right-hand fingering options shown.

# THE MAJOR SCALE

The notes of the musical alphabet (sometimes called the *natural notes*) have the following arrangement of whole and half steps:

```
A   B   C   D   E   F   G   A
 W   H   W   W   H   W   W
```

| W = Whole Step |
| H = Half Step |
| ∨ = Whole step |
| ‿ = Half step |

A *scale* is an ordered group of notes played one after the other, either ascending or descending, in a specific pattern of whole and half steps. They always move through the musical alphabet in order. Most scales contain seven different notes, and finish with the same note on which they began. This starting and finishing note is called the *tonic*.

The most important scale in our musical tradition is the *major scale*. A major scale results from playing eight notes in alphabetical order with the following sequence of whole steps and half steps:

For example, here is the C major scale:

### Ex.32

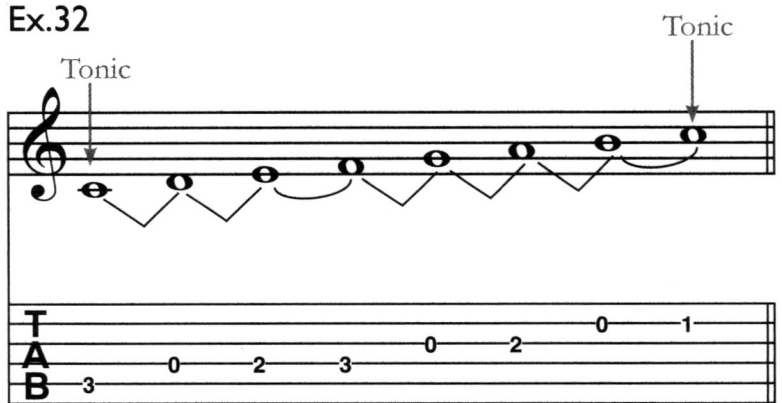

Because of the sequence of whole and half steps that exists in the musical alphabet, a C major scale just happens to involve no accidentals. If we start on a tonic other than C, we will have to alter at least one note with either a sharp or a flat to make the sequence of whole and half steps conform to that of the major scale.

## Good vs. Bad Crosses

Before beginning to play scales, it is important to understand the two different ways we cross strings. In a good cross, we move from a lower string to an adjacent higher string with *i* crossing to *m*, or *m* crossing to *a*. For example, when crossing from the 3rd to the 2nd string, a good cross would have *i* finish on the 3rd and *m* begin on the 2nd. A bad cross would go from *m* to *i*. Try both, and you'll immediately see why we call one "good" and the other "bad." Bad crosses require a lot more movement from the arm. We must become fluent in both types of crosses. Practice these exercises before going on.

Ex.33

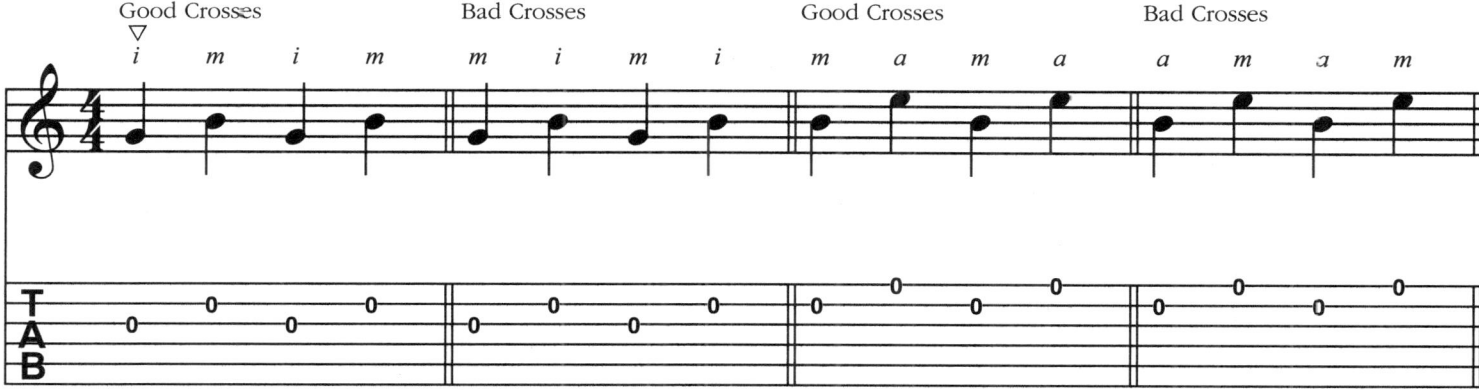

## THE G MAJOR SCALE

Ex.34

Here is a G major scale. Play it using *i–m* alternation in rest stroke. At first, it is a good idea to pause at every string crossing to make sure the arm is doing its job and that your hand and finger positions are remaining constant. Remember that your fingers should move simultaneously in opposite directions, and that there should be no pedaling-style movements. Try all four finger alternations shown.

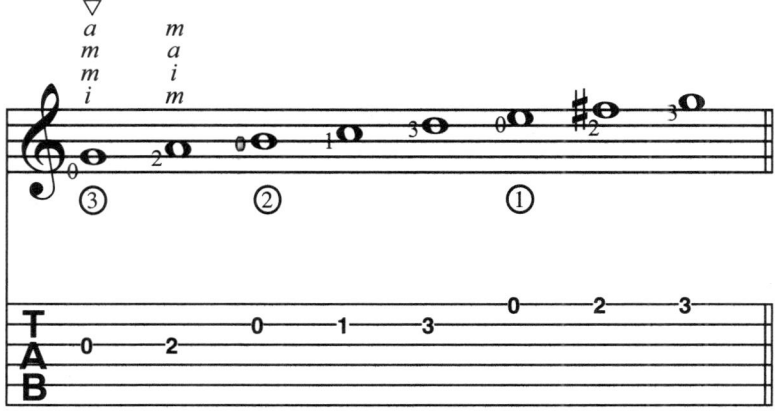

## PLAYING MAJOR SCALES ON ONE STRING: SHIFTING

On page 52 you used your knowledge of whole steps, half steps, and the musical alphabet to locate and label all the natural notes on the guitar fingerboard. Now that you know about major scales, it will be easy for you to play a major scale on one string. This will further develop your knowledge of the guitar fingerboard, and give you additional shifting practice. Have fun!

Use *p* free strokes to play the E, A, and D major scales. Alternate *i* and *m* in rest stroke for the G major scale. Pause as necessary at shifts until you are confident that you can do them easily, smoothly, lightly, and with accuracy.

**E Major on the 6th String.** (Use *p* free stroke.)

Ex. 35

**A Major on the 5th String.** (Use *p* free stroke.)

Ex. 36

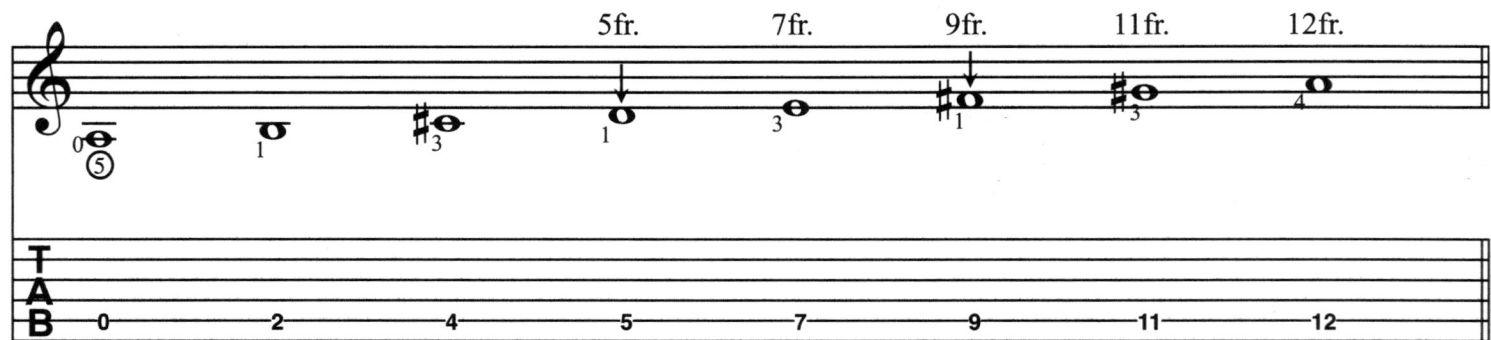

**D Major Scale on the 4th String.** (Use *p* free stroke.)

Ex. 37

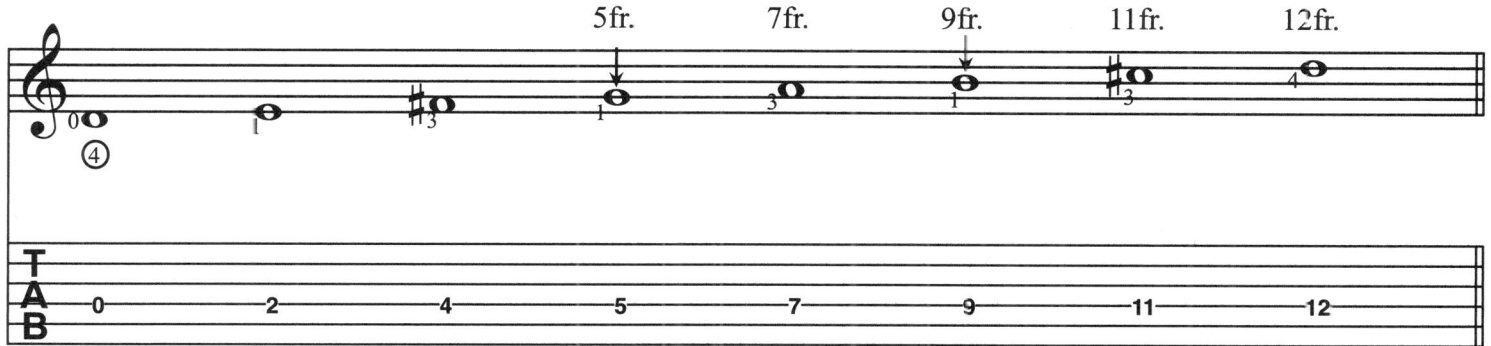

**G Major Scale on the 3rd String.** (Alternate *i* and *m* rest strokes.)

Ex. 38

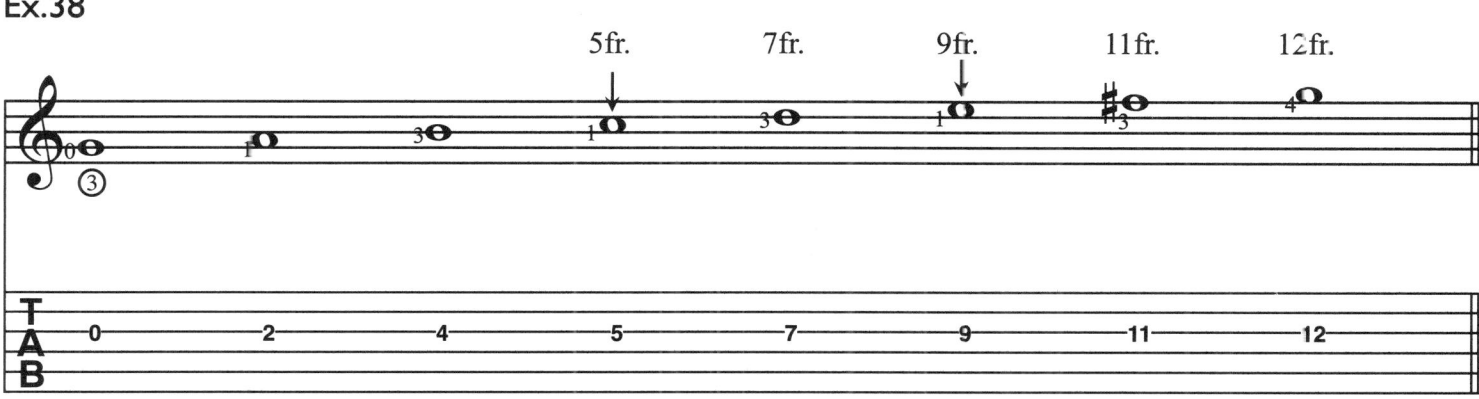

## Mauro Giuliani

*Probably one of the most brilliant guitar virtuosi ever to have lived, Mauro Giuliani was born in 1781 and died in 1829. His fame was such that the first classical guitar magazine ever published, in 1833, "Giulianiad," was named for him. He was born in Italy, but died in Vienna, where he spent most of his career. It was Giuliani's excellence that inspired Beethoven to say that "The guitar is a miniature orchestra in itself." Giuliani composed over 300 works for guitar.*

# Introducing High A, B, C, D, and E on the 1st String

Your shifting technique will allow you to learn some higher notes on the 1st string. These notes have ledger lines above the staff. Since each looks uniquely different from the others, they are easy to read. A has one ledger line, B sits just above one ledger line, C has two, D sits just above the second ledger line, and E has three.

**High A** is on the 5th fret of the 1st string. Use your 1st finger.
**High B** is on the 7th fret of the 1st string. Use your 3rd finger.
**High C** is on the 8th fret of the 1st string. Use your 4th finger.
**High D** is on the 10th fret of the 1st string. Use your 1st finger.
**High E** is on the 12th fret of the 1st string. Use your 3rd finger.

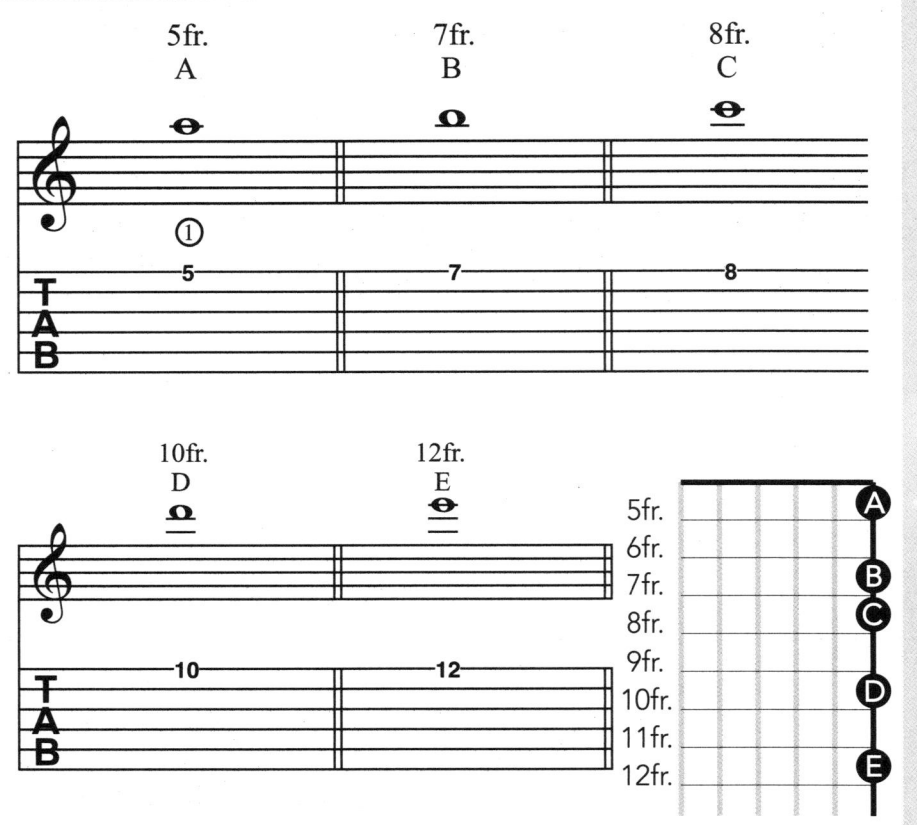

The actual choice of which finger to use on any note is based on the context. We may choose one over another for the sake of ease, or for a smoother sounding connection between the notes. The fingerings suggested above are just there to get you started. Assume that you will always be evaluating fingering choices.

Alternate *i* and *m* rest strokes in Examples 39, 40, and 41.

### Ex.39

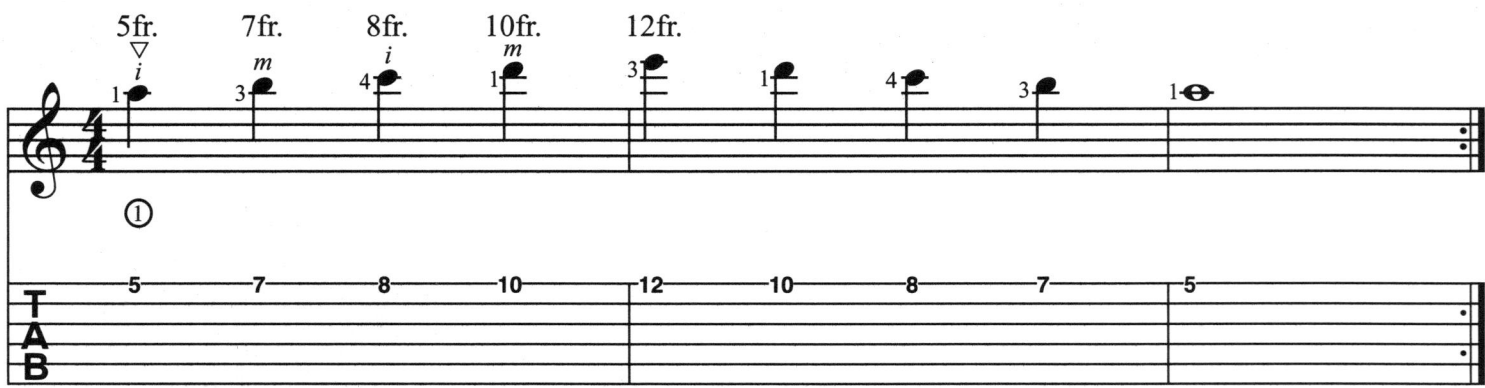

**B Major Scale on the 2nd String.** (Alternate *i* and *m* rest strokes.)

Ex.40

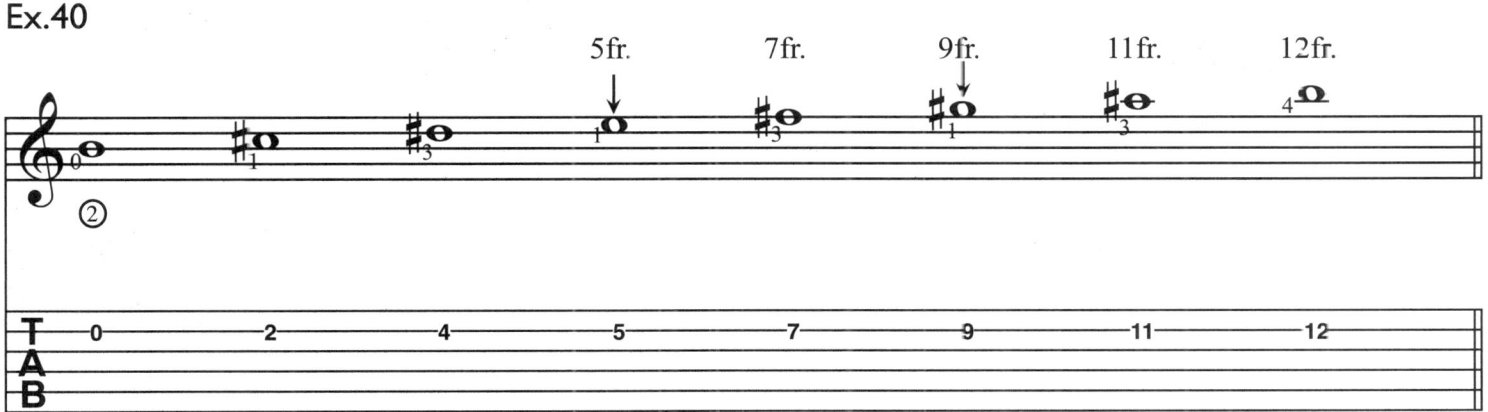

**E Major Scale on the 1st String.** (Alternate *i* and *m* rest strokes.)

Ex.41

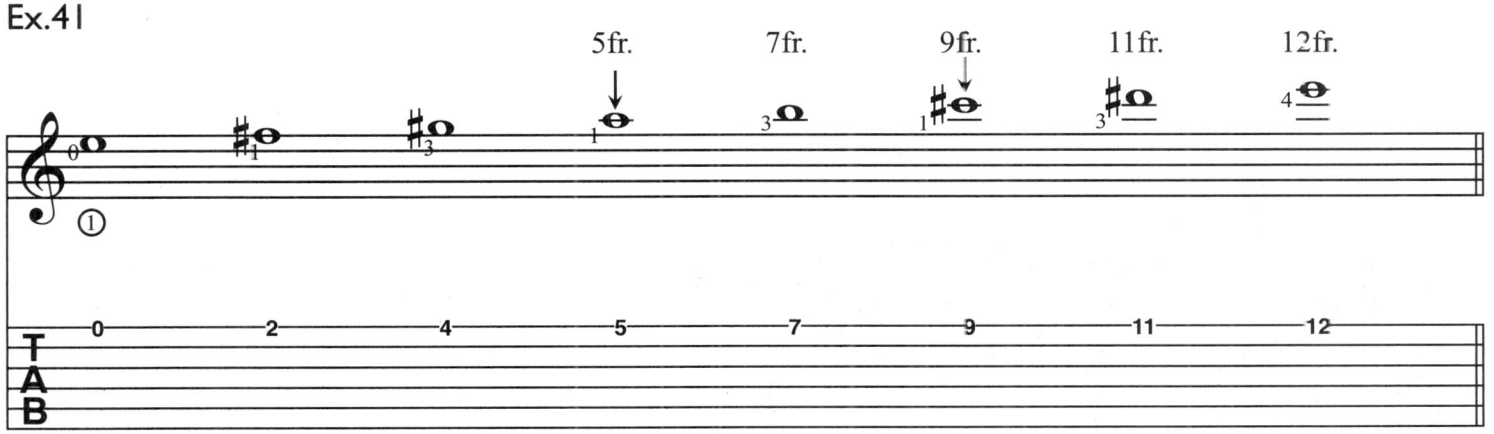

## Francisco Tárrega

*Francisco Tárrega (1852–1909) was an important Spanish composer whose music and guitar playing became very influential in the 20th century. Considered by many to be "the father of modern guitar playing," he was central to reviving the guitar as a solo instrument in recital and concerts. Among his most popular compositions are "Recuerdos de la Alhambra" and "Danza Mora." He wrote nearly 80 original works for the guitar and over 100 transcriptions, mostly of piano pieces by Chopin, Beethoven, and others.*

# PIECES USING REST STROKE AND *p*

As a warm-up, practice Example 31 on page 51, alternating *i* and *m* in rest stroke, inserting *p* strokes between the two finger strokes. When this is easy for you, proceed to the pieces and enjoy!

## Sakura      Track 64

"Sakura" is a traditional folk melody from Japan. Yuquijro Yocoh wrote a set of variations on it for classical guitar, which John Williams recorded. This beautiful tune is a favorite among students of classical guitar.

Traditional Japanese Melody

## Introducing the Dotted Eighth, Sixteenth Rhythm

## Variation on a Minuet by José Ferrer      Track 65

At [A], and throughout the piece, there is a dotted eighth note-sixteenth rhythm. Counting "1-e-&-ah," you would play on "1" and "ah." At [B], be sure to hold the C in the treble through the G bass note. At [C], hold the F# in the bass for the whole measure. This is your most challenging project, yet. Learn the notes with the stems down, then the notes with the stems up before putting them together.

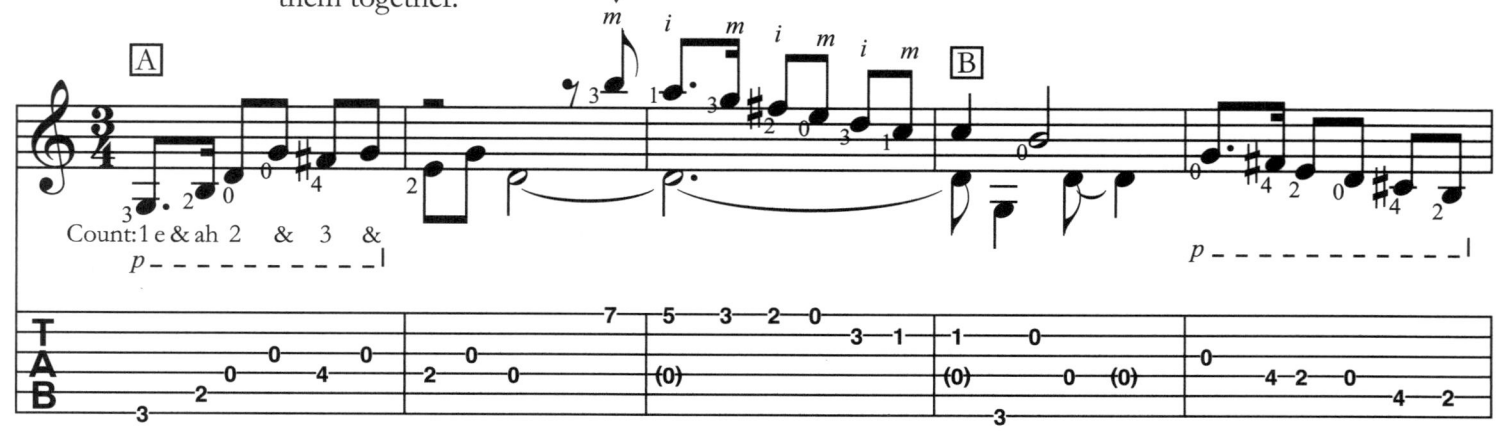

TEACH YOURSELF TO PLAY CLASSICAL GUITAR 59

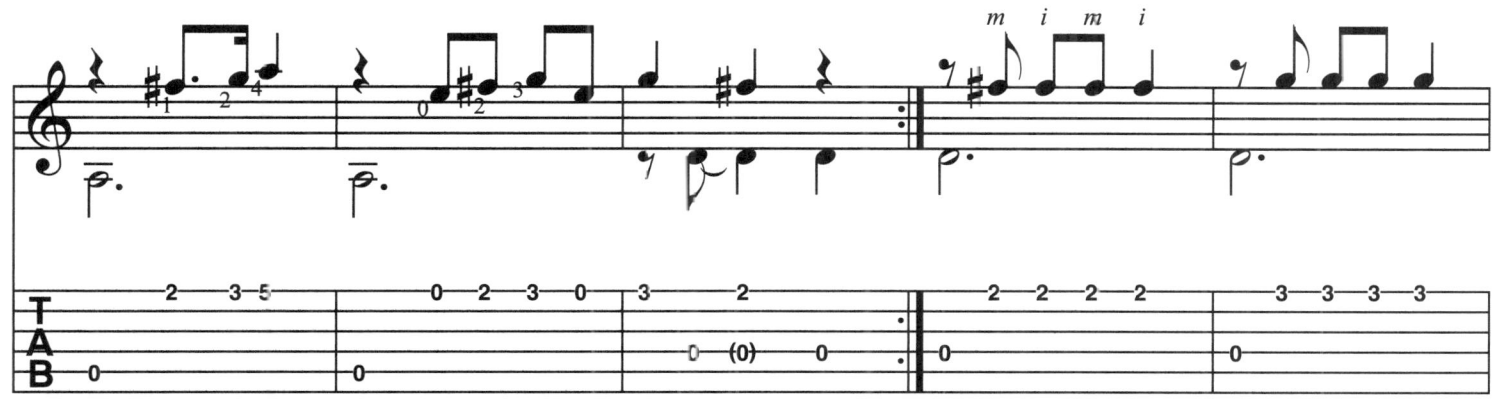

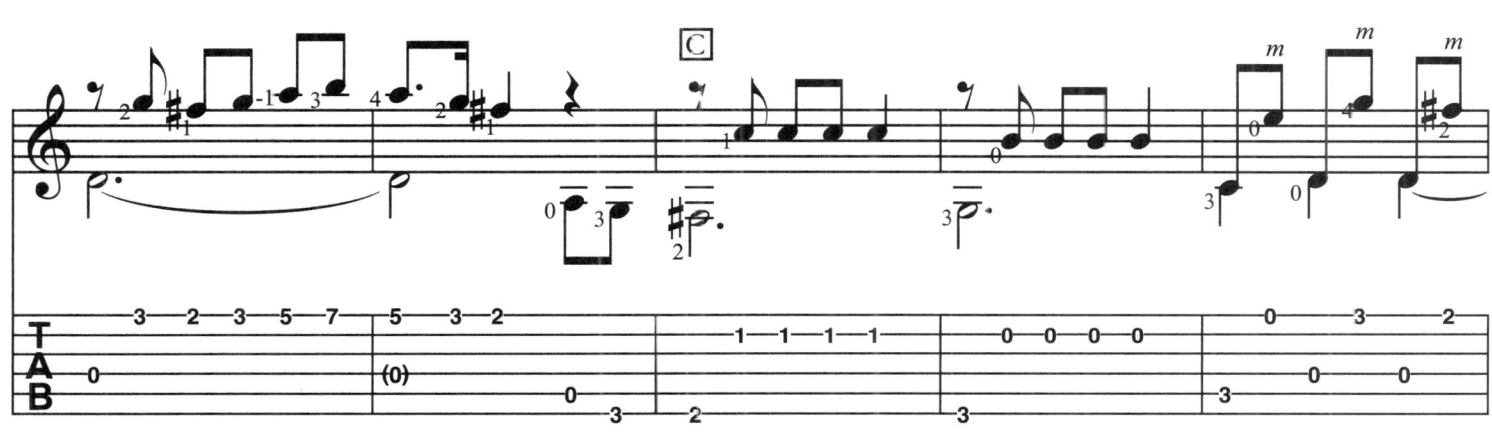

# CHORDS AND ARPEGGIOS

As you learned on page 23, a chord is two or more notes played together. The most common type of chord involves three notes and is called a *triad*. For example, if we put the tonic of a major scale together with the 3rd and 5th steps above it, we get a *major triad*.

Ex.42

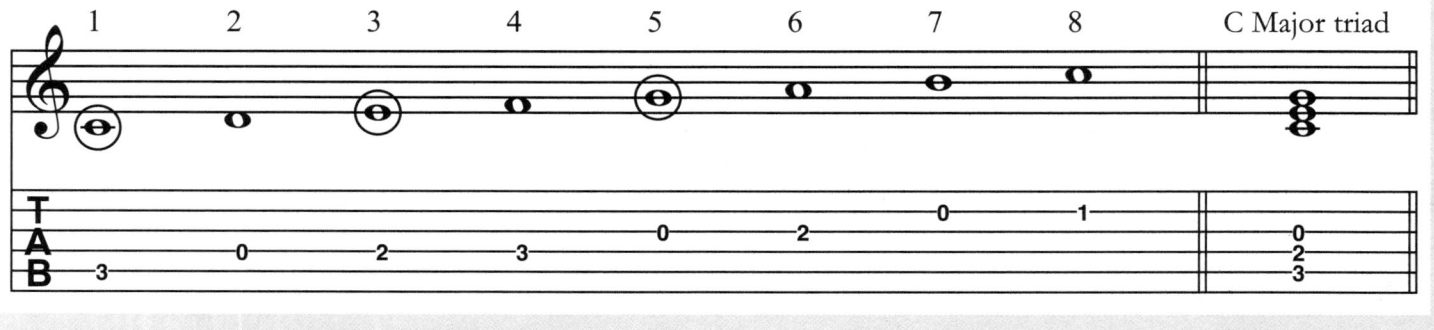

## IMPORTANT

There are other types of triads, and it is very important for you to learn about them. Get a good theory workbook, such as Aaron Shearer's *Elements of Music Theory for Guitar* (Alfred FC02321), and work through it. Also, get a good chord book such as Robert Brown's *Ultimate Guitar Chord Bible* (Alfred 40289) and start learning all the open position chord forms (avoid barre chords at first). Strum through some pop or folk songs. A surprising suggestion? Some classical music lovers may be wincing as you read this, but playing chords will give your left hand a good workout (as long as you avoid playing with difficulty) and increase your general knowledge of the guitar.

### Napoleon Costé

*Born in 1806, Costé was one of the greatest guitar virtuosi that France has ever produced. Along with his contemporary, J. K. Mertz, Costé's music was rediscovered in the 20th century. In 1860, he fell after a concert and broke his arm. He never performed publicly again, but when he died in 1883, he left behind a legacy if virtuosic, romantic music. He also invented a guitar that was larger than usual and was tuned a 5th lower. In addition, it had a fingerboard that extended over the soundboard.*

# Arpeggios

An *arpeggio* is a broken chord. In other words, the notes of a chord are played one at a time. Arpeggios are most often played entirely in free stroke, and are one of the most idiomatic musical gestures for guitar. That is to say, arpeggios are very guitaristic; they are easy for us to play, and they are very musically satisfying, too, since they make the guitar sound great.

There are two basic categories of arpeggios: *simple* arpeggios, where there are no finger alternations, and *compound* arpeggios, where one or more finger alternations are required. This book will just introduce the simple arpeggios.

## The *p–i–m* and *p–m–i* Arpeggios

The most important aspect of simple arpeggio technique is that there are no finger alternations. The fingers play one at a time, but they follow each other in order as they play, and extend together, as for a chord.

Prepare *i* and *m* on the 3rd and 2nd strings respectively, as for a two-note free-stroke chord. You should have *p* in the at-rest position against the tip of *i*.

Step 1. Play and follow-through with *i*, keeping *m* on its string. Then hold *i* inside the palm.
Step 2. Play and follow-through with *m* (remember to move *a* and *c*, too), slowly and smoothly extending *p* directly to the 5th string.

Step 3. Play the 5th string with *p*, simultaneously releasing *i* and *m* together to their respective strings.

The arrows in Example 43 show where the alternations between thumb and fingers occur in this arpeggio.

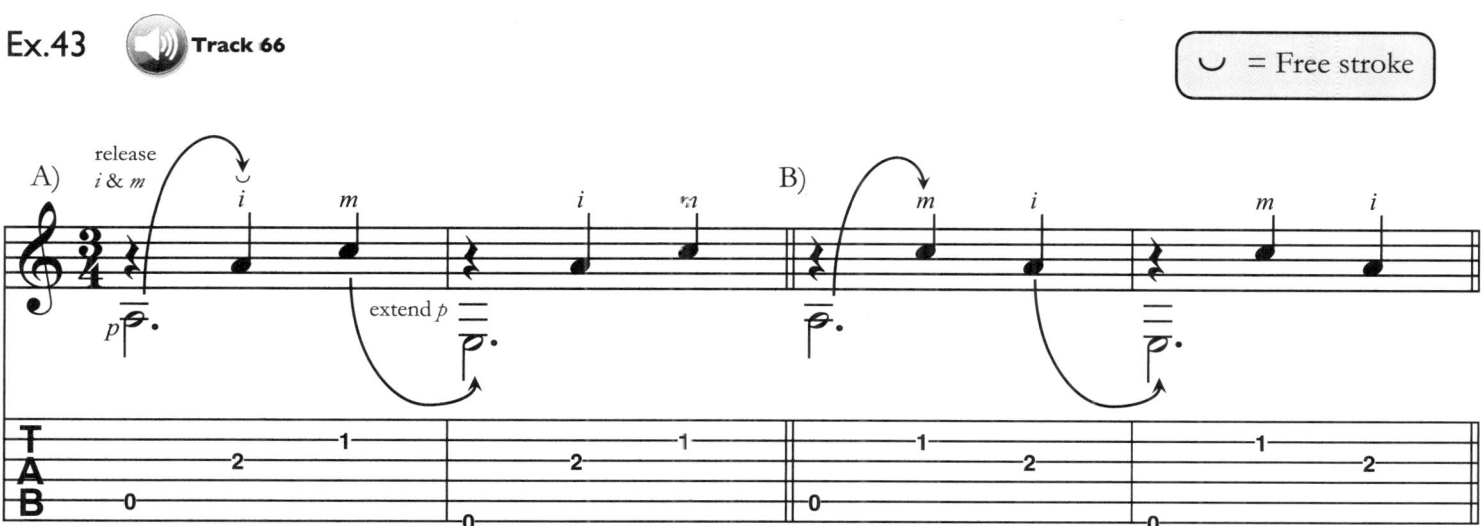

If you play *m* first, followed by *i*, extending *p* as *i* plays, you will have the *p–m–i* arpeggio.

As always, strive to keep your hand still and in position. The procedure described above involves always preparing the fingers on the strings before playing. As you become more confident, try releasing the fingers to a point just in front of the strings—not stopping the last notes from ringing before you play. Just make sure the finger that plays last remains below its string while the other one plays. Fingers like to follow each other around—it's anatomically natural for them. That's one reason arpeggios are easy for us. But we have to refine this natural tendency so the fingers follow each other in a controlled way, with the timing we want. So, when playing the *p–i–m* arpeggio, you may have to work at keeping *m* from jerking in when *i* plays. Make the effort. The extra concentration this requires will pay off in speed and fluency

# ARPEGGIO STUDIES FROM GUILIANI'S 120 RIGHT-HAND STUDIES

Written in the first part of the 19th century, Mauro Giuliani's *120 Right-Hand Studies* have stood the test of time as among the most important exercises for classical guitar students.

### Training the Left Hand

The following studies have some three-note combinations for the left hand that may seem awkward at first. Learn them slowly. Try to develop a plan for the movements between the chords. Move gracefully and slowly. If a movement is timed well—starts at the earliest possible moment and moves no faster than is necessary to arrive at the new note at precisely the right time—it will be smooth and easy. Generally, left-hand movements are only difficult and "jerky" looking when they are mistimed. Think of your left-hand fingers as dancers, and develop a beautiful choreography for them. Remember that in an arpeggio, although you must ultimately hold down all of the notes of a chord together, your fingers can arrive on their notes one at a time. You don't have to grab them all at once. That's just one more reason why arpeggios are a great guitar technique!

## INTRODUCING TRIPLETS

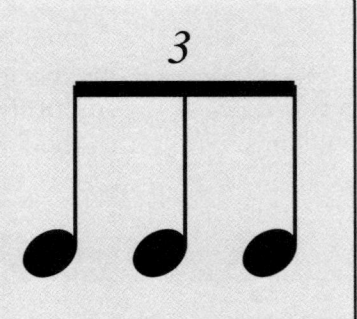

When three notes are grouped together with the figure "3" above or below the notes, the group is called a *triplet*. The rhythmic value of the triplet is equal to the value given to two of the same kind of note.

In $\frac{3}{4}$ or $\frac{4}{4}$ time, two eighth notes get one count, so an eighth-note triplet will also get one count.

Ex. 44  Track 67  Giuliani No. 2

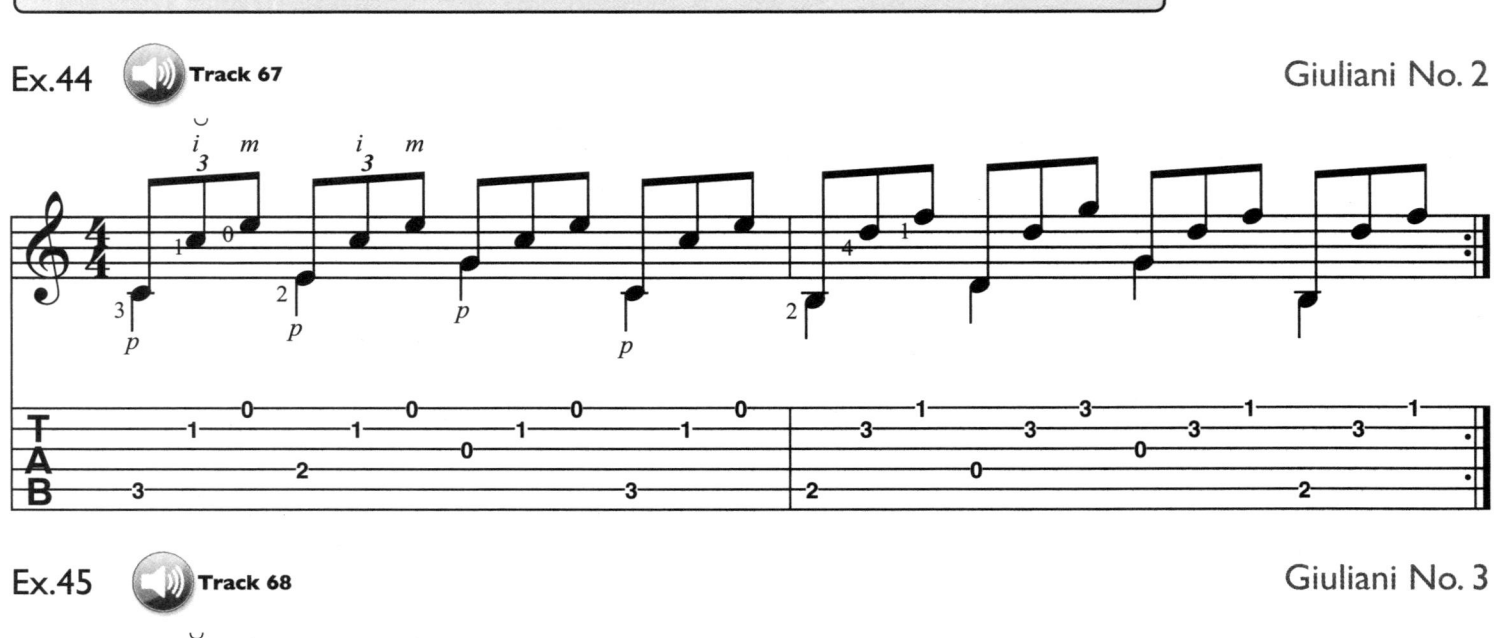

Ex. 45  Track 68  Giuliani No. 3

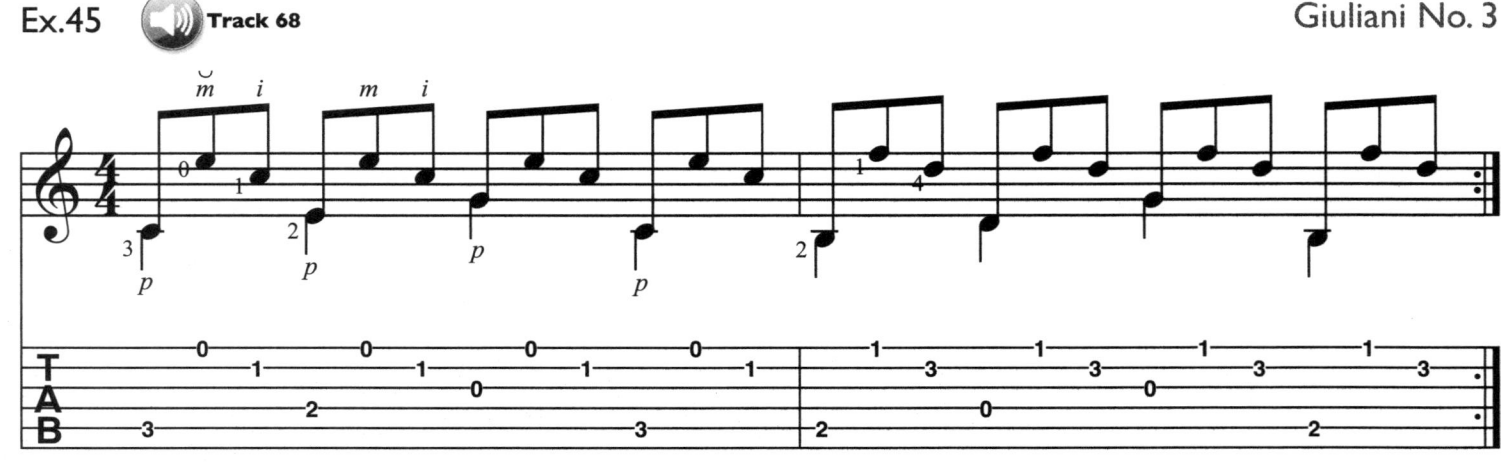

## INTRODUCING DYNAMICS

The most basic expressive tools we have are *dynamics*, which have to do with how loudly or softly we play. If we strike the strings with more energy, they will sound louder. If we strike them more gently, they will sound softer. Here are the basic terms used to describe dynamics:

| | | |
|---|---|---|
| *p* | *piano* | soft |
| *mf* | *mezzo forte* | medium loud |
| *f* | *forte* | loud |
| *ff* | *fortissimo* | very loud |

## Three-Note Chords with *i–m–a*

Three-note chords are played just like two-note chords, but we add *a* to the mix. Place *i*, *m*, and *a* on the 3rd, 2nd, and 1st strings. Check your free-stroke position with each finger. Keeping your hand still and in position, push through the strings towards the palm of your hand.

Remember that *c* (the pinkie) should follow *a*, so all four fingers will move into a light fist.

**On the 1st, 2nd, and 3rd Strings**

Ex. 48 Track 71

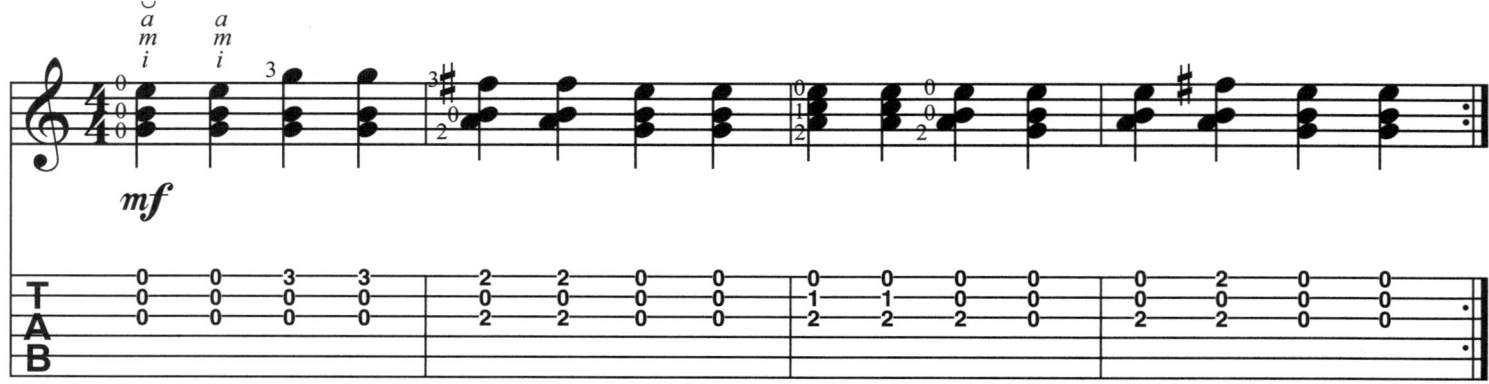

**On the 2nd, 3rd, and 4th Strings**

Ex. 49 Track 72

Cross your arm up (move towards the ceiling) to position the fingers for these strings.

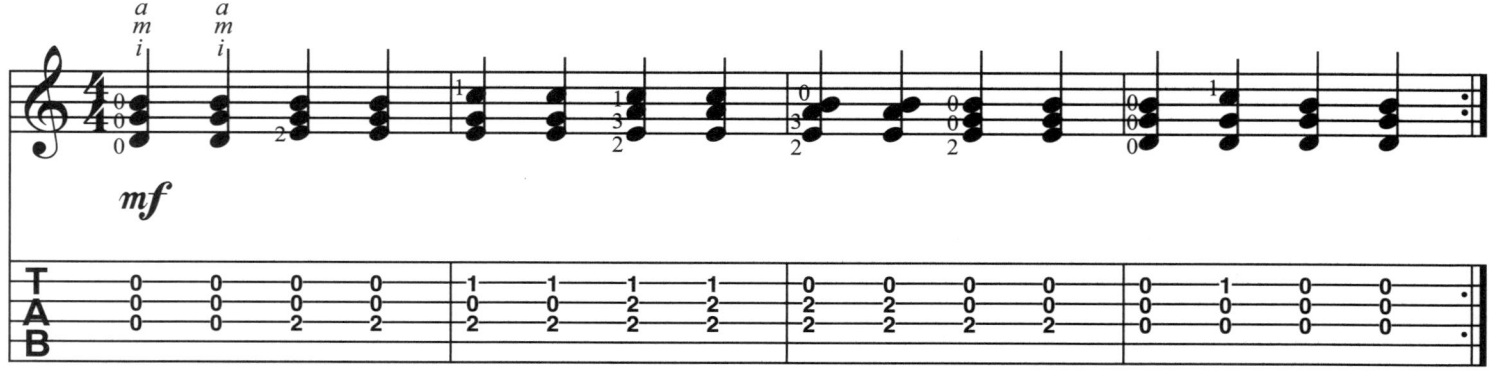

Ex. 50 Track 73

Now try alternating three-note chords with *p*.

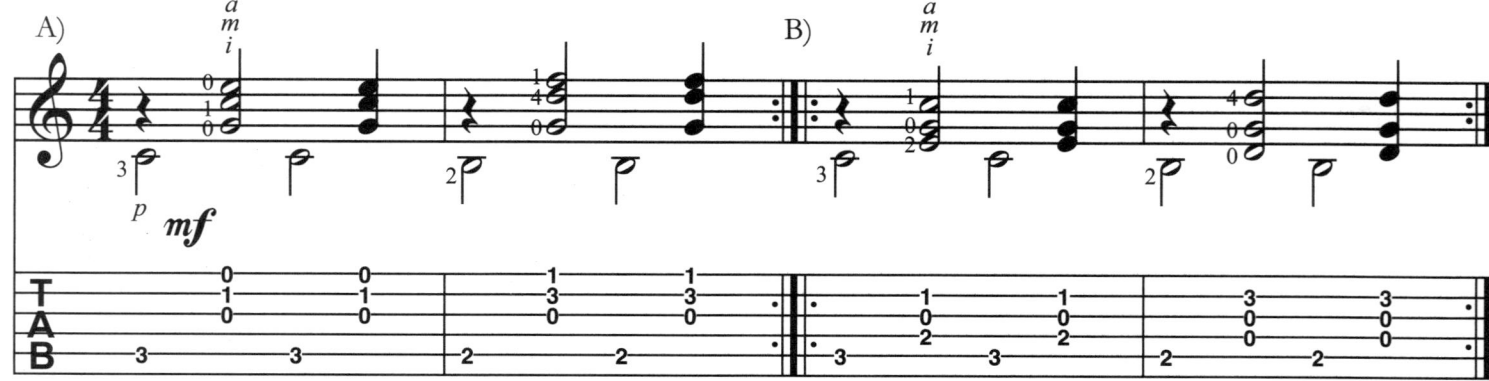

# The *p–i–m–a* and *p–a–m–i* Arpeggios

Simple arpeggios involving *a* simply take the idea of *p–i–m* and *p–m–i* arpeggios one step further. Prepare *i*, *m*, and *a* on the 3rd, 2nd, and 1st strings as for a three-note chord and rest *p* against the tip of *i*.

Step 1. Play and follow through with *i*, keeping *m* and *a* on their strings. Then hold *i* inside the palm.
Step 2. Play and follow-through with *m*, keeping *a* on its string. Hold *i* and *m* inside the palm.

Step 3. Play and follow-through with *a*, slowly and smoothly extending *p* directly to the 5th string.
Step 4. Play the 5th string with *p*, simultaneously releasing *i*, *m*, and *a* together to their respective strings.

Ex.51  Track 74

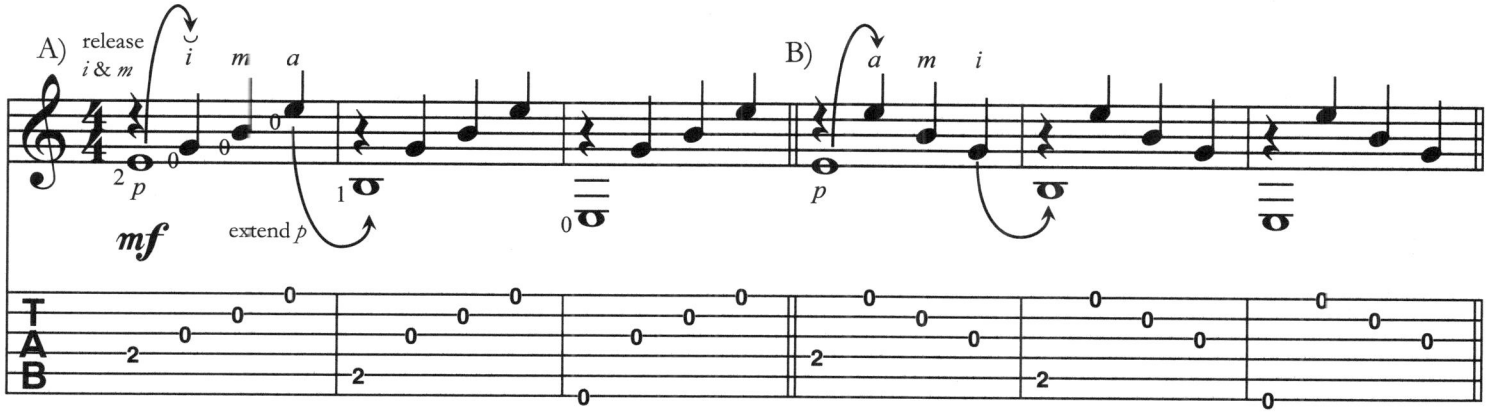

If you play *a* first, followed by *m* and then *i*, extending *p* as *i* plays, you will have the *p–a–m–i* arpeggio.

When this feels comfortable, try not preparing the fingers on the strings before they play. This is where things get a bit trickier, since *a* does not have much natural independence from *m* and will try to jerk in when *m* plays. Until you develop good finger independence, you will have to exert a fair amount of energy to keep the middle joint of *a* still when *m* plays. If you get at all tired, stop! Practice a little at a time until you build endurance. The "no pain, no gain" attitude has caused injury to countless musicians.

### IMPORTANT
Exaggerate the *a* middle joint extension in the *p–i–m–a* arpeggio when not preparing on the strings. It will help you develop the finger independence you need.

## INTRODUCING TEMPO SIGNS

> The three principal *tempo signs* are **Andante** (slow), **Moderato** (moderately), and **Allegro** (fast).

## SUPPLEMENTAL PIECES

### Variation on a Study by Dionisio Aguado  Track 78

Practice carefully (prepare, repeat, and review!), make good left-hand choreographies, and have fun!

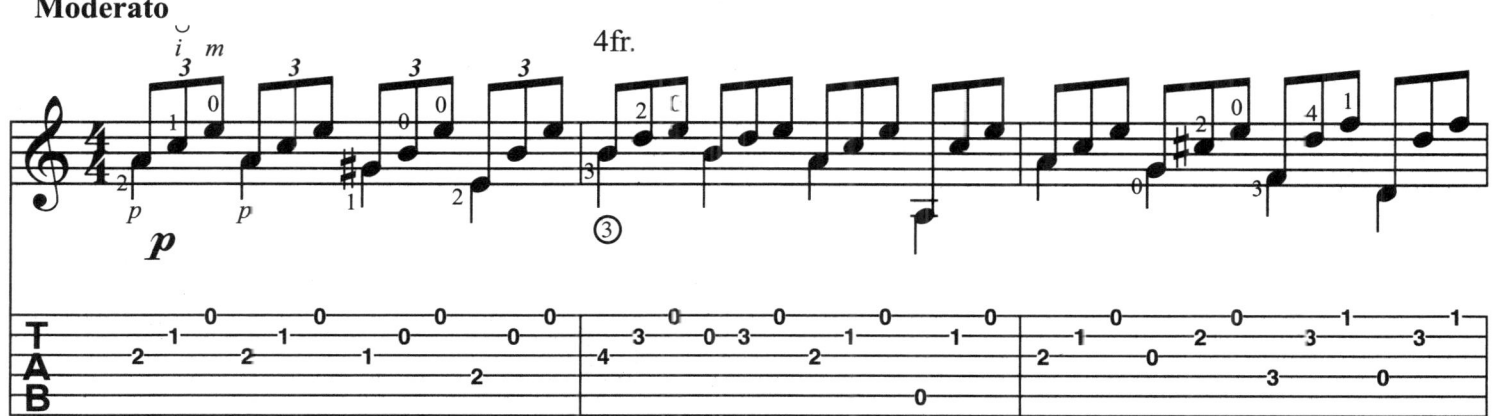

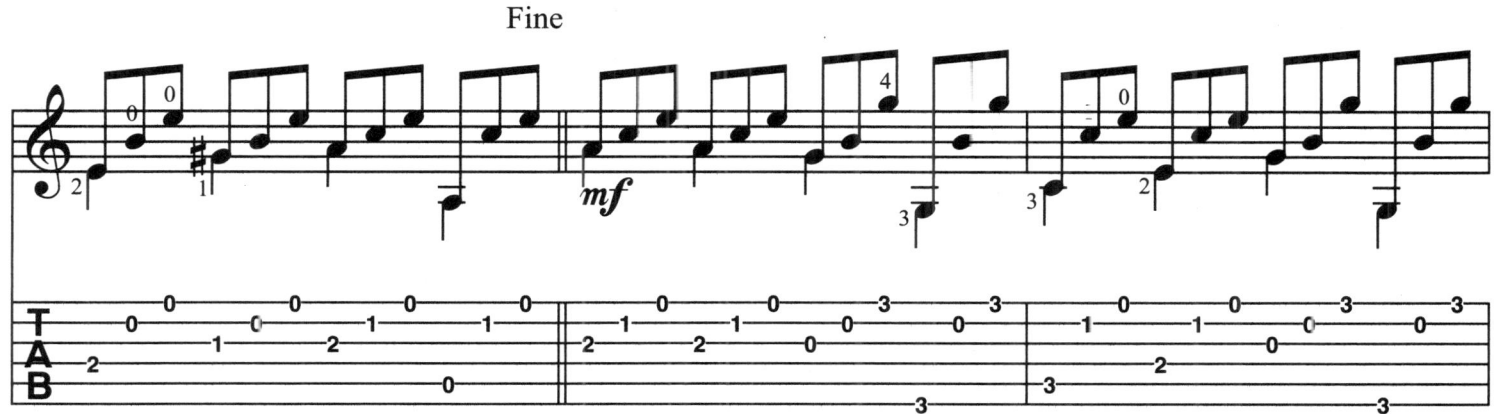

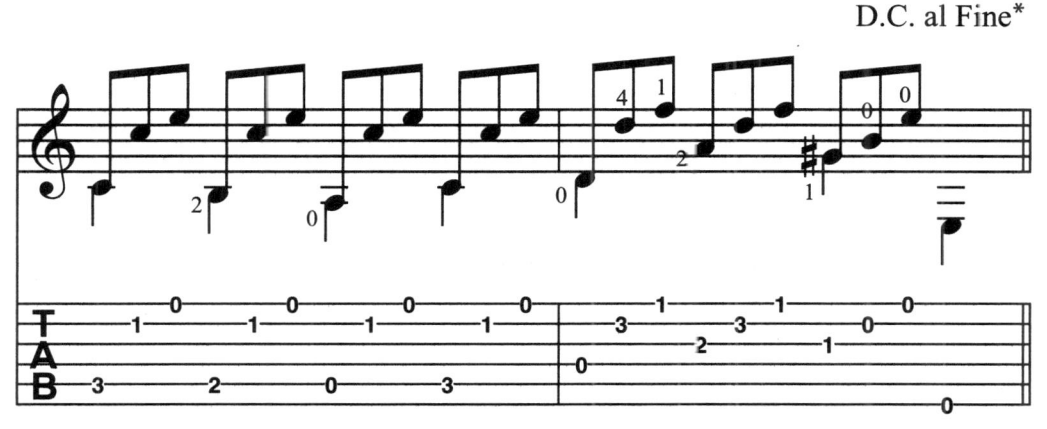

> \* *Da Capo al Fine.*
> Return to the beginning and play to the *Fine*. In Italian, "*capo*" means "head" and "*Fine*" means "the end."

## Key Signatures

*Key signatures* appear at the beginning of every staff. They tell us which notes are sharp or flat in a piece. In the popular classical guitar melody that follows, an F♯ and a C♯ appear in the key signature. That means every F and C in the piece is played as a sharp unless marked with a natural sign ♮.

## Largo from the Concerto in D Major    Track 79 Both Parts   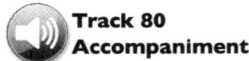 Track 80 Accompaniment

You can play the "Largo" with a string orchestra accompaniment that comes with the audio for this book. *Largo* is an Italian word meaning slow and stately.

At [A], use a *barre* (hold two or more strings with one finger) to finger the C♯ and F♯ at the same time. Barres are often indicated with a Roman numeral to show the fret, and a small Arabic numeral to show how many frets are being barred. To do a barre, lay the left side of your 1st finger across the 1st and 2nd strings at the 2nd fret.

by Antonio Vivaldi

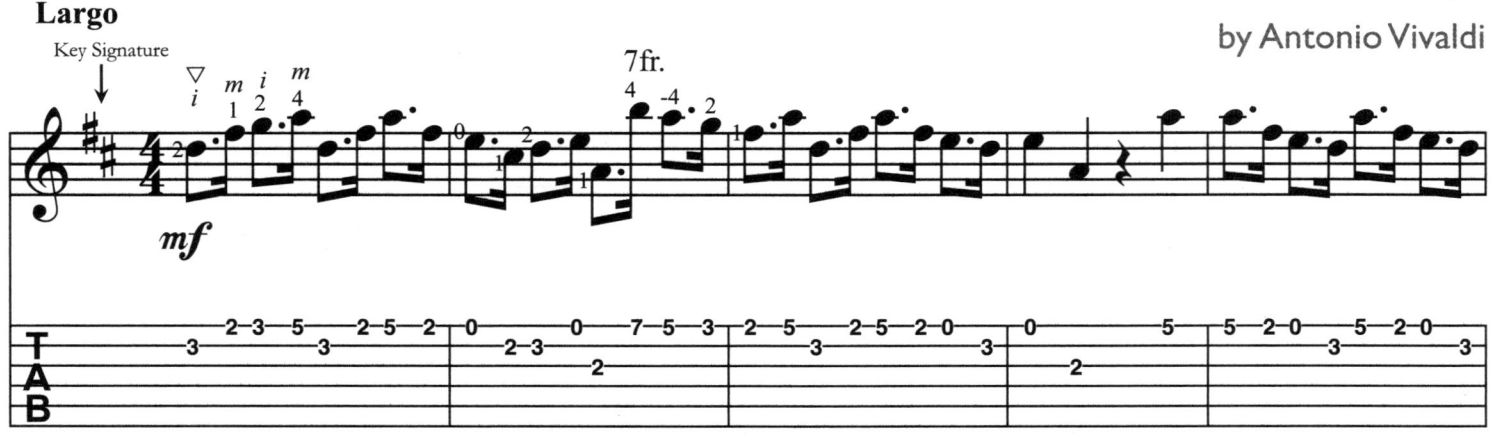

# TEACH YOURSELF TO PLAY CLASSICAL GUITAR 69

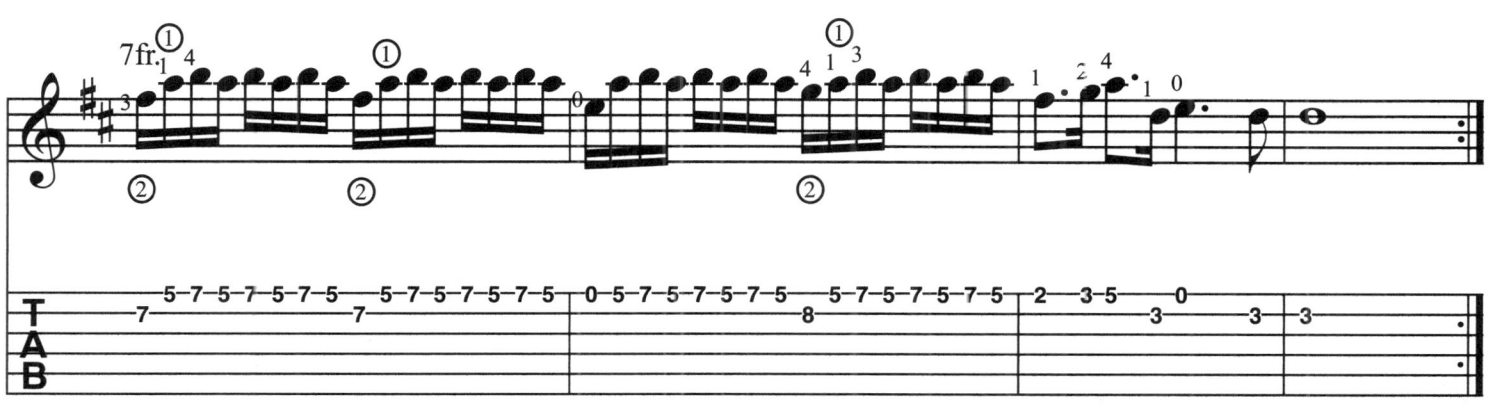

### More Dynamic Signs

This sign is a *crescendo*. It means "getting gradually louder" and is abbreviated as *cresc.*

This sign is a *decrescendo*. It means "getting gradually softer" and is abbreviated as *decresc.*

# Lullaby

by Johannes Brahms

In "Lullaby," you will play the fingers simultaneously with the thumb. Keep the hand steady and try to balance the energy between them. The music is written in three voices: *bass* (stems down), *treble*, stems up, and a light chordal accompaniment (stems down). You will notice some rests in the middle while bass and treble play. Note the dynamic markings. Also, notice the *arpeggiation* sign ⸦ in the third full measure. It tells us to *roll* the chord by planting the fingers and quickly pulling them across the strings in succession.

**Andante**

\* *Dolce* is Italian for "sweet" so play with a lot of expression.

The first time through, play through this *1st ending*, go back to the beginning and play again.

The second time, skip the 1st ending and play the *2nd ending*, instead.

\*\* This curved line is called a *descending slur*. Only the first note is plucked, while the other notes are performed by pulling the left-hand fingers off the string in a slightly forceful way to sound the notes without plucking. They are often marked with a "P" in the TAB, for *pull-off*. These notes are *thirty-second notes* (three beams) and are twice as fast as sixteenth notes.

# Country Dance  Track 82

Carulli's "Country Dance" sounds beautiful and is satisfying to play. It also puts together many of the concepts you've learned in this book. At A, B, and C make sure the fingers follow each other as in an arpeggio. Also note the intentional repeated right-hand fingerings in measure 3. This is to set up the right-hand fingering in the next measure.

by Fernando Carulli

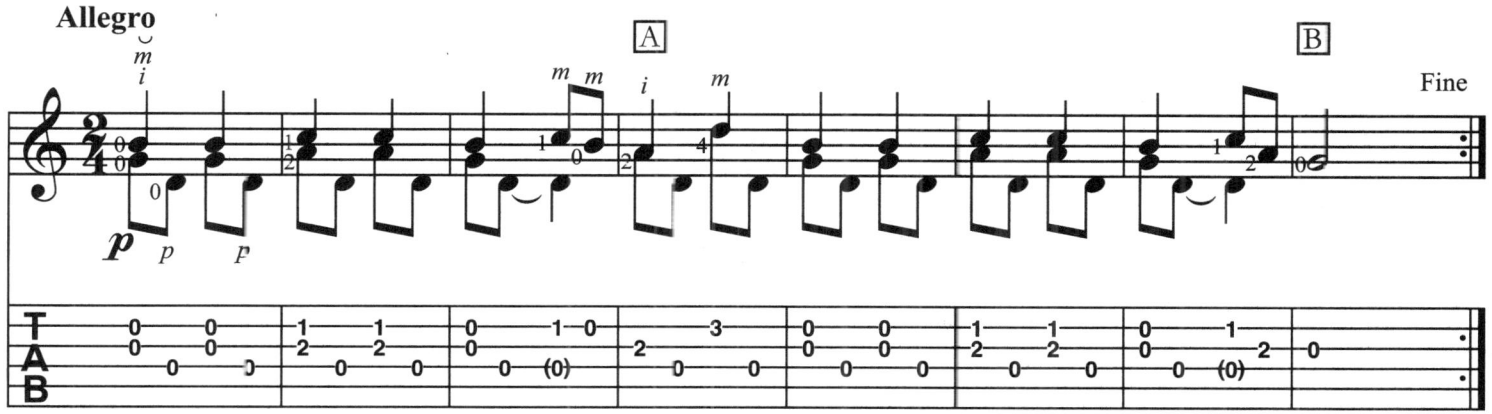

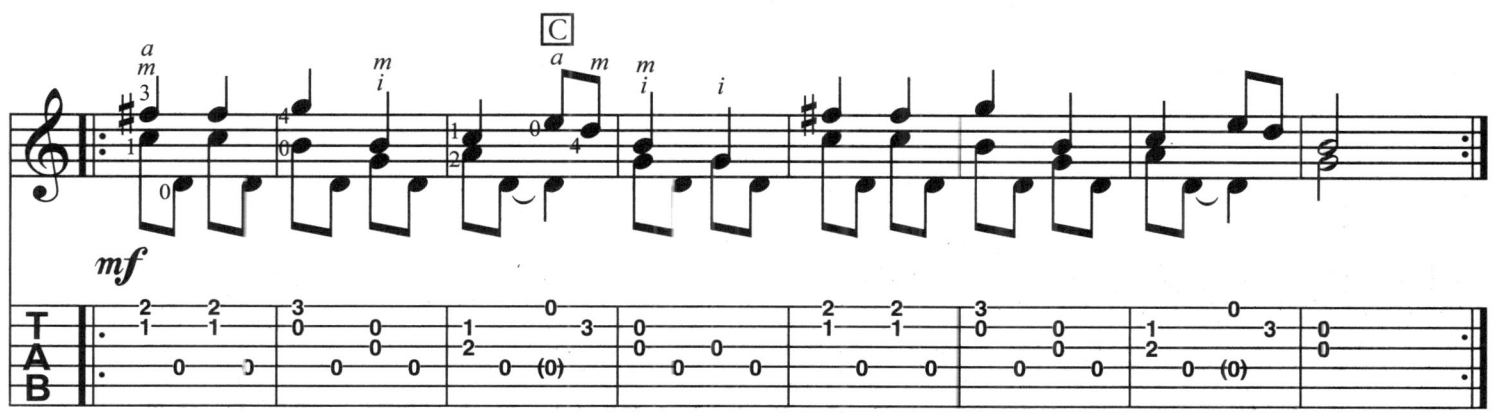

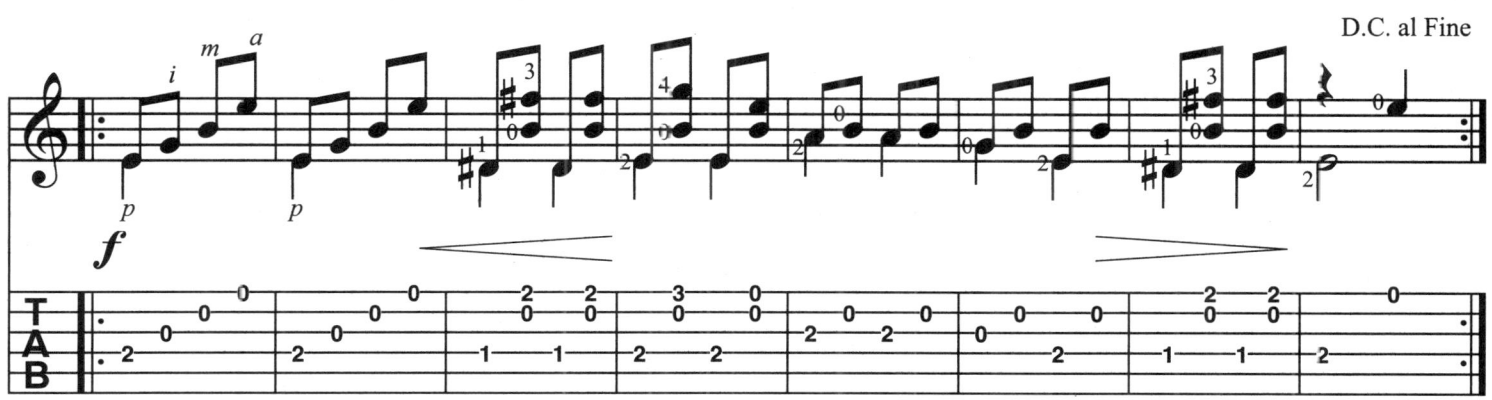

# Minuet in G  by Johann Sebastian Bach

This "Minuet" features embellishments on the 2nd-string C called *inverted mordents* (✹). We use *slur* technique to perform these. Play the written note, pull the finger off to sound the open B without plucking, then hammer the finger back on to re-sound the C, again, without plucking. Near the end of the piece, we find a *mordent* (✹) on the open B string, which is the exact opposite: play the written note, hammer on the 1st finger to sound the C without plucking, then pull it off to re-sound the B.

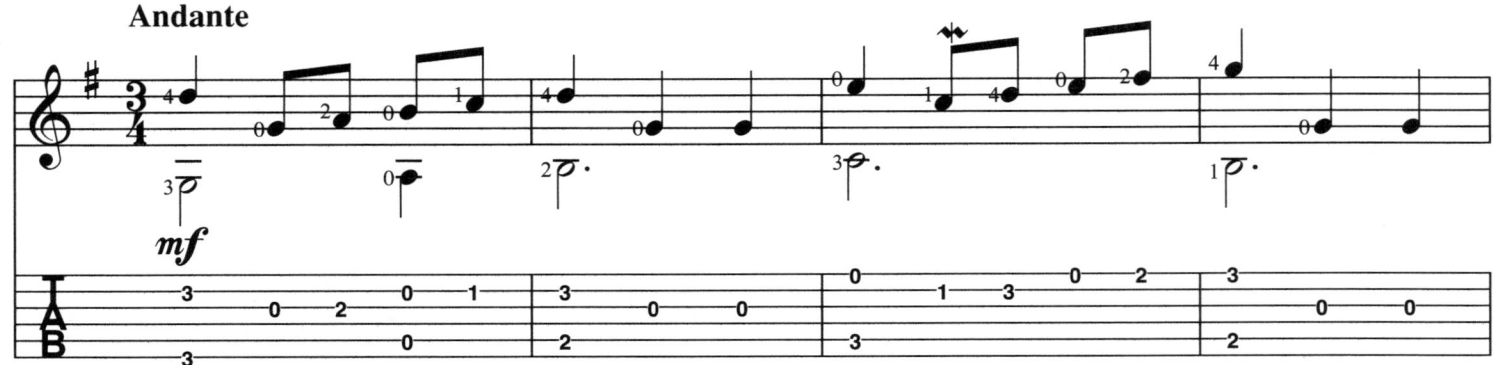
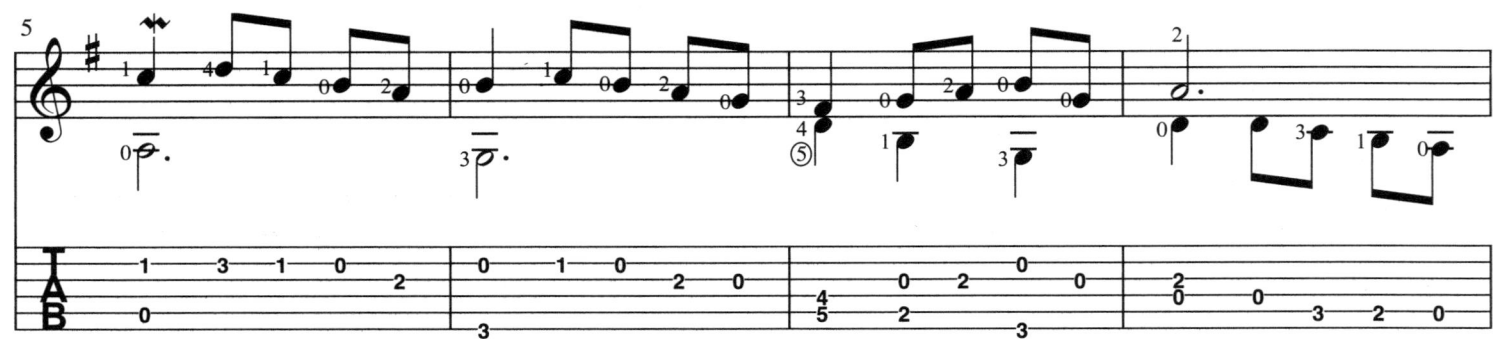
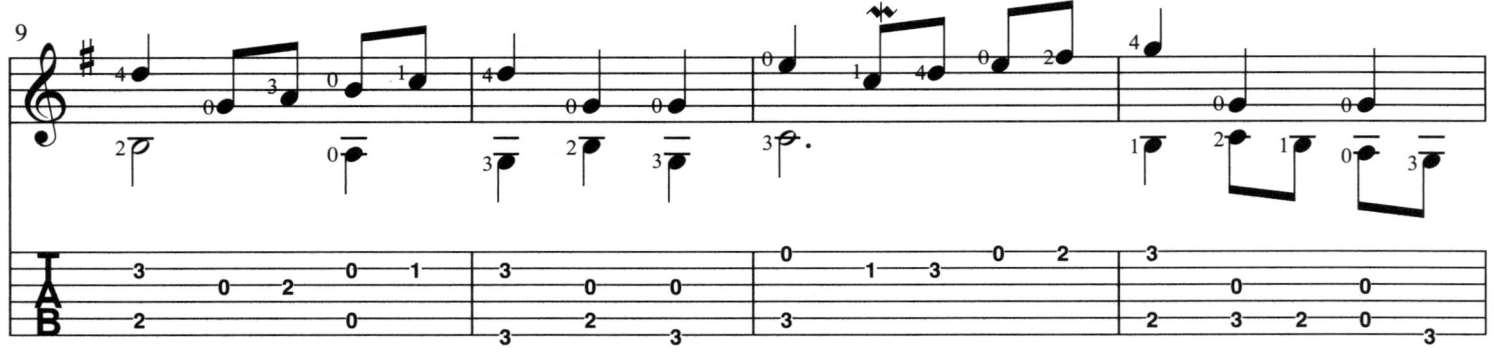
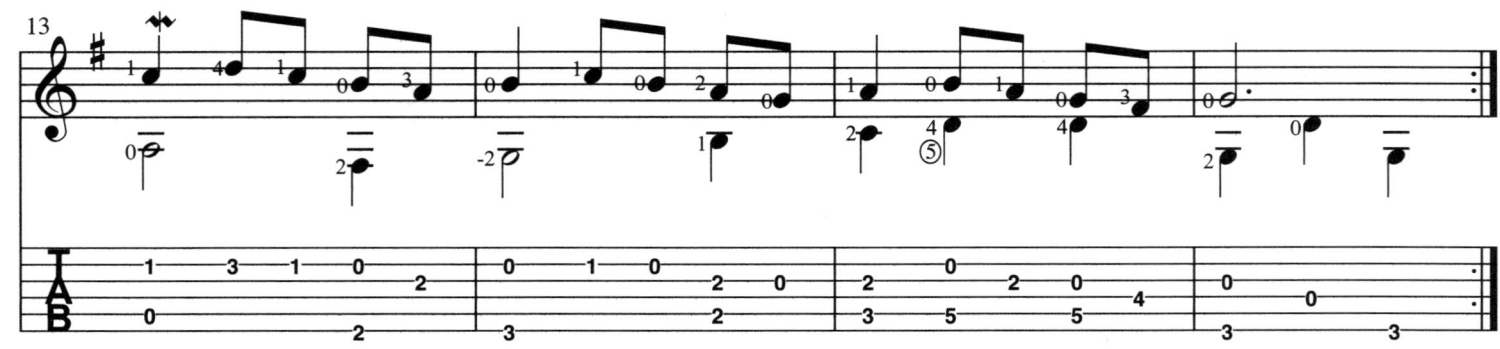

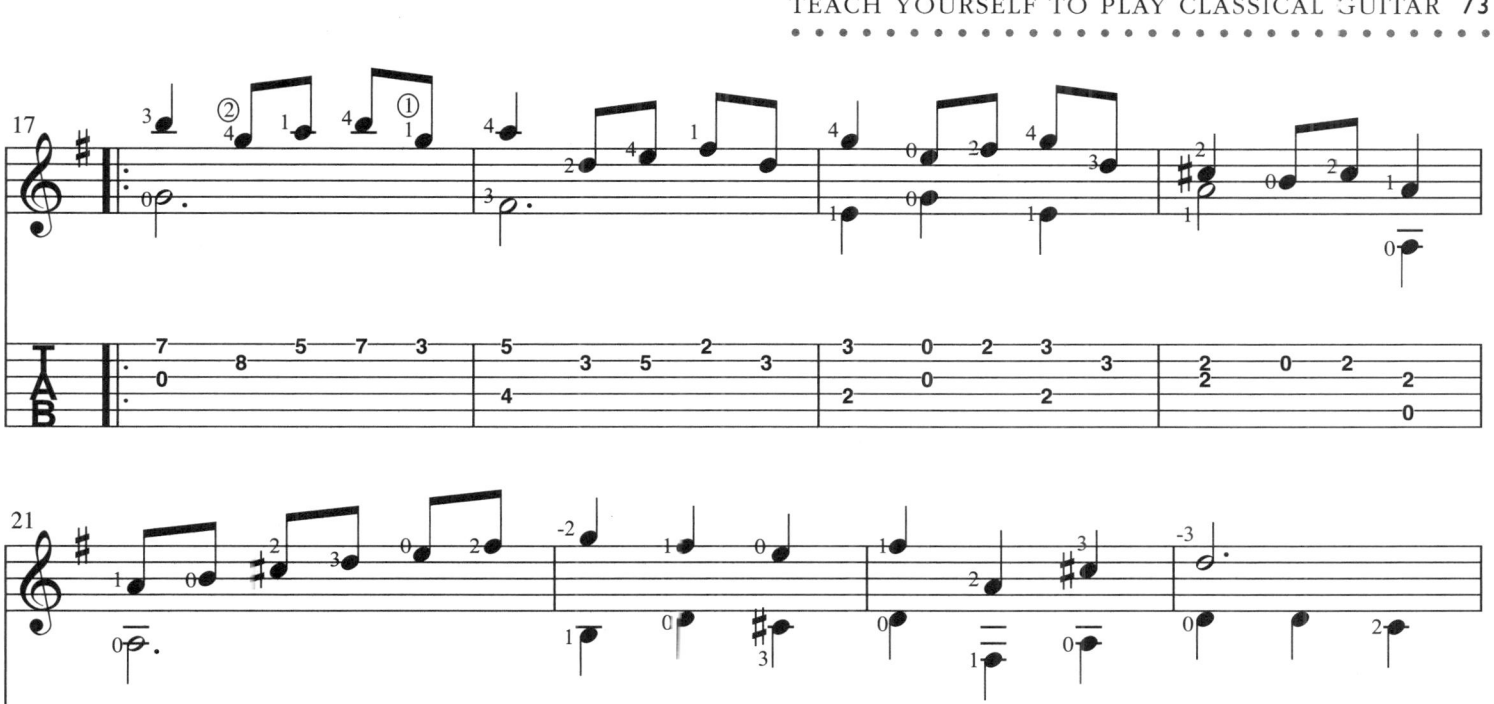
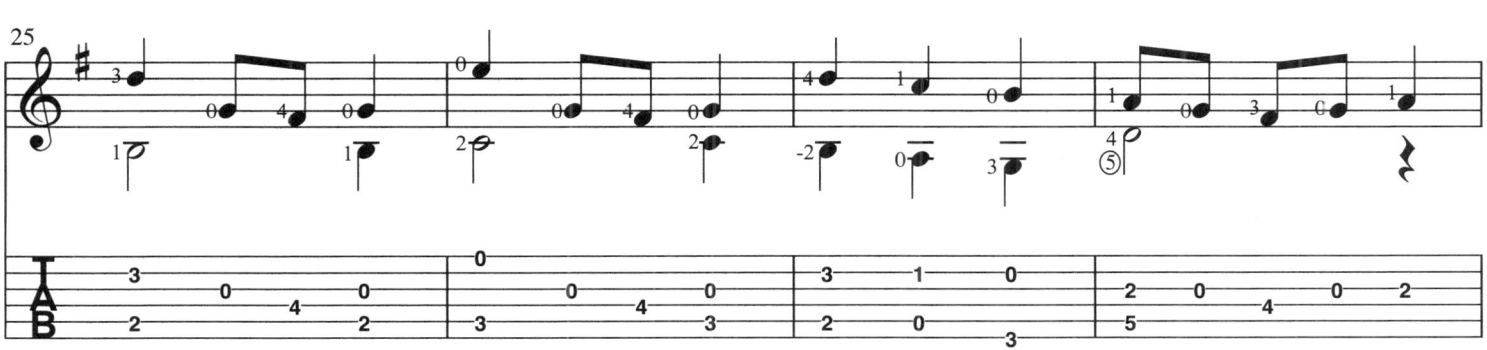
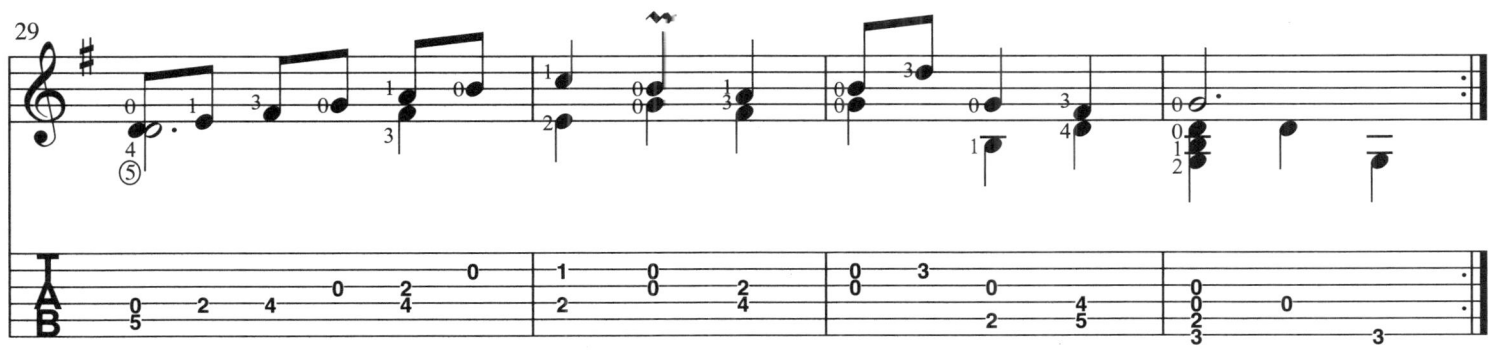

### THREE- AND FOUR-NOTE CHORDS

Some of the pieces in this section include three- and four-note chords where *p* and the *i*, *m*, and *a* fingers play free stroke simultaneously. Strive for a balance of pull between the fingers and thumb so the right hand remains still, and the notes in the chords sound equal. Be sure to follow through toward the palm, and use the knuckle joints in the finger strokes.

### Introducing the Sixteenth Rest

 A *sixteenth rest* indicates silence for one quarter of a beat.

# Humoresque  Track 84

This light-hearted, graceful piece is very challenging but fun to play. *Andante grazioso* means in a graceful, walking tempo, and *leggiero* means "lightly." In measure 16, the *rit.* indication means *ritard*, or "gradually slowing down." Then, *a tempo* means to return to the same tempo as the beginning.

**Andante grazioso**

by Antonín Dvořák

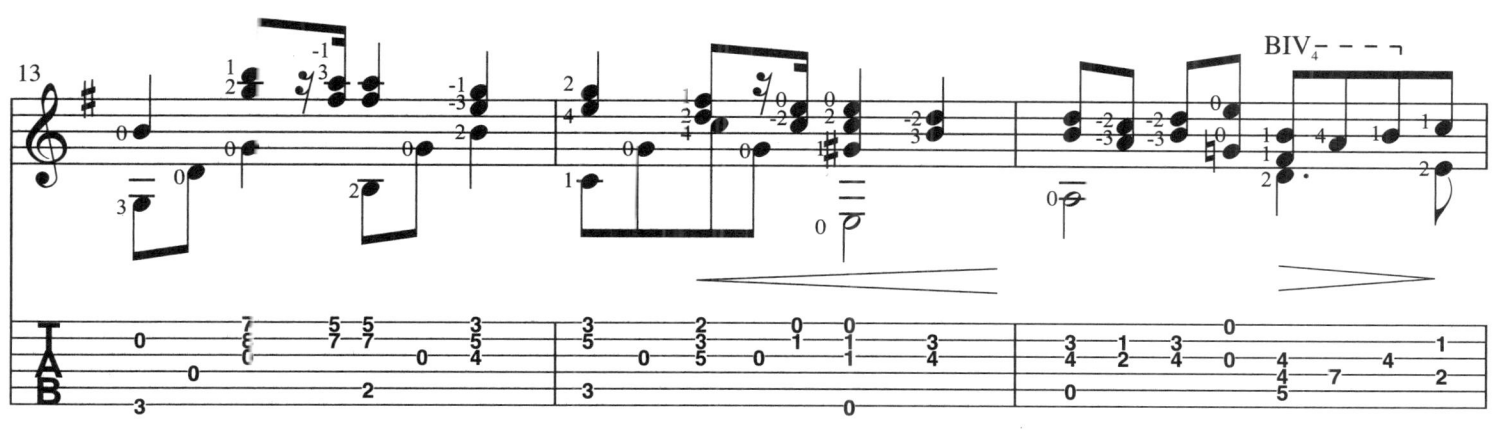

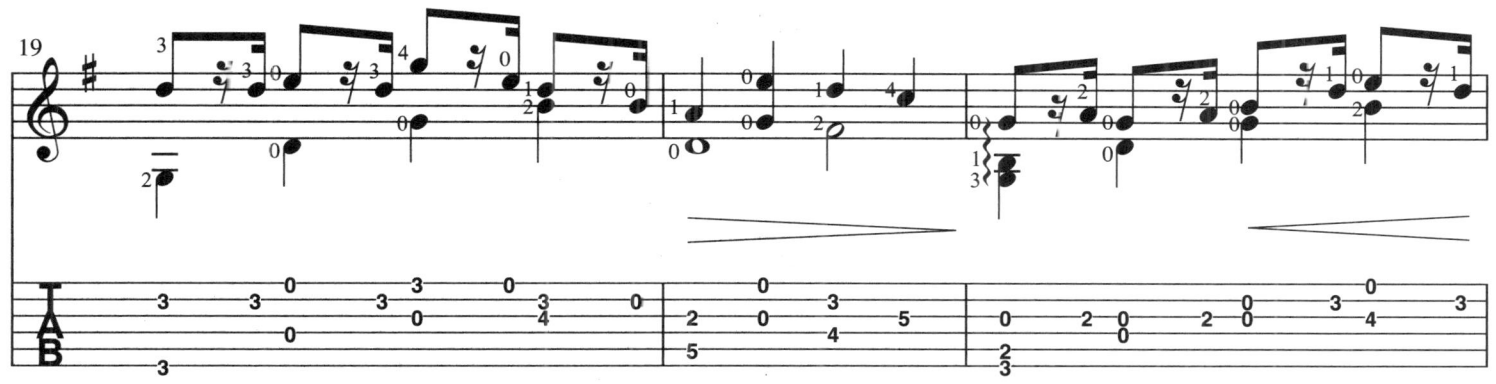
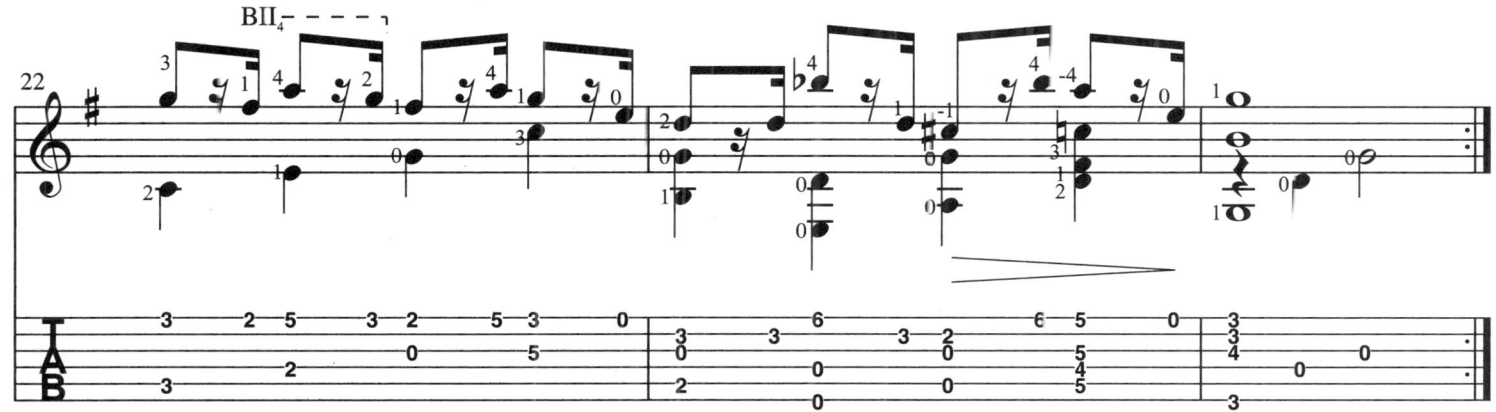

# Eine kleine Nachtmusik: Romanze

 Track 85

by Wolfgang Amadeus Mozart

Notice the dots over some of the notes. These indicate *staccato*, which means to shorten the note. How short the note is played is a matter of taste and context. Since this is not a fast piece, the staccato notes will not be terribly short.

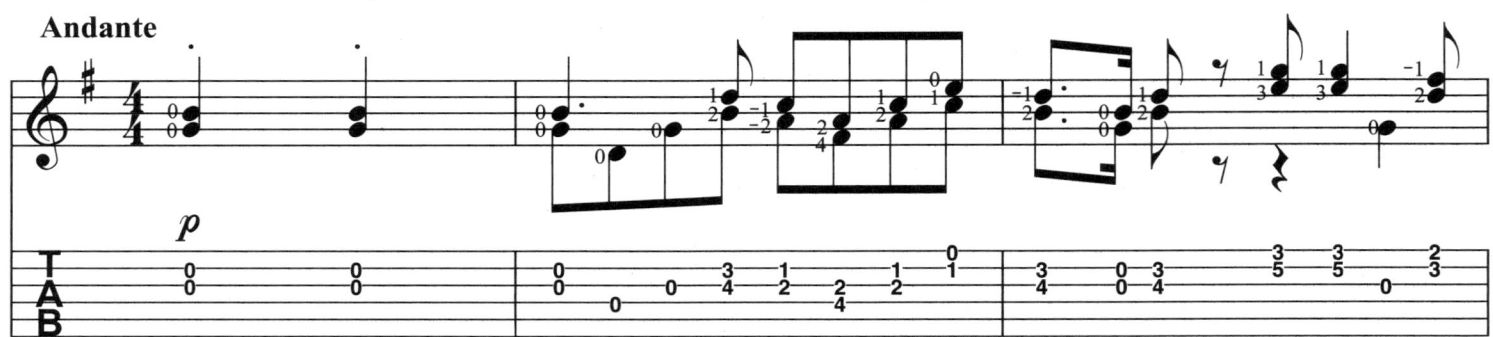

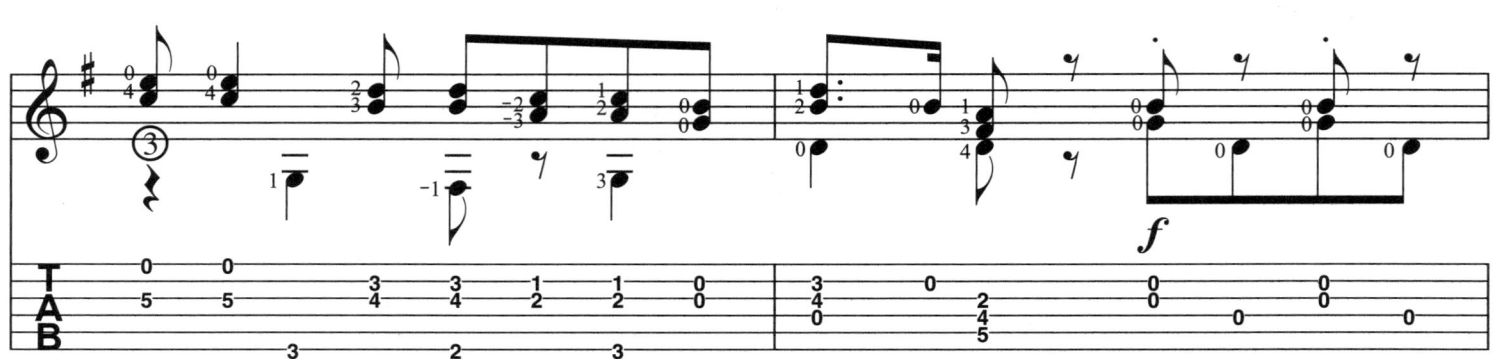

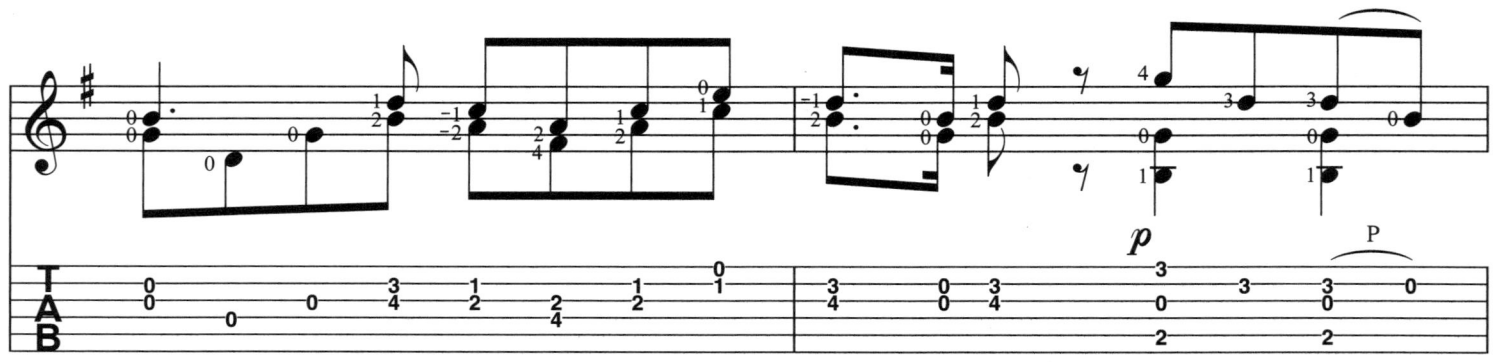

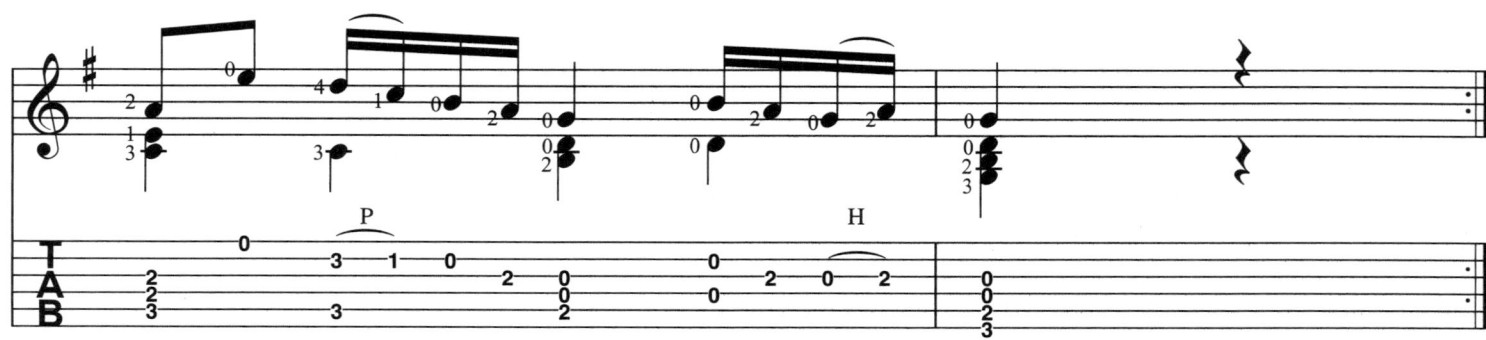

* This curved line is called a *ascending slur*. Only the first note is plucked, while the following note is performed by hammering the left-hand fingers down on the string in a slightly forceful way to sound the note without plucking. They are often marked with a "H" in the TAB, for *hammer-on*.

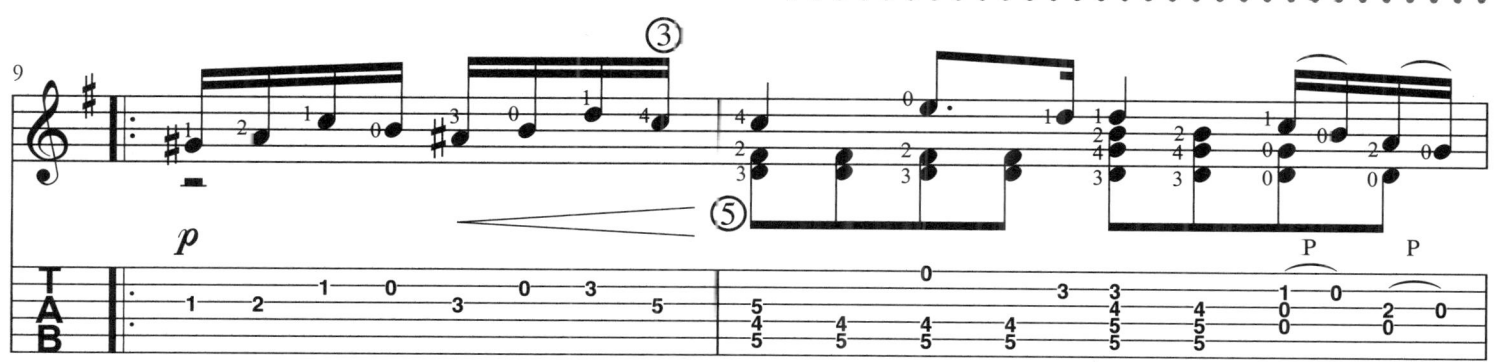
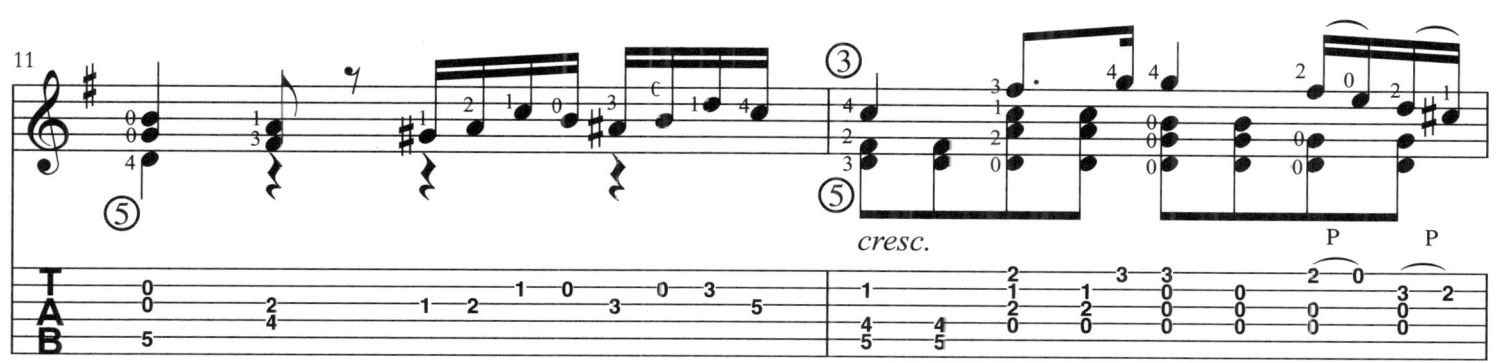
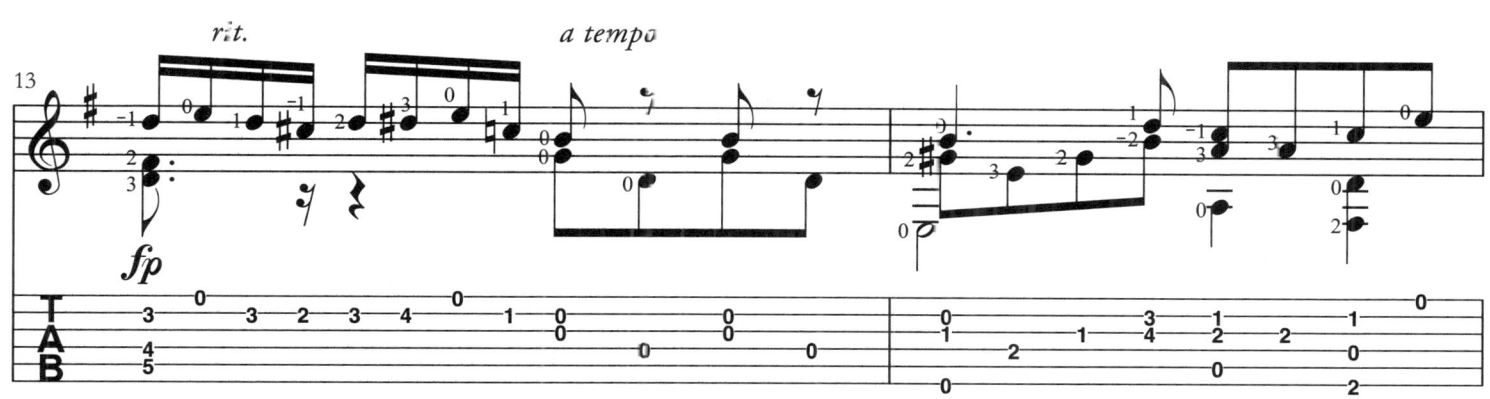
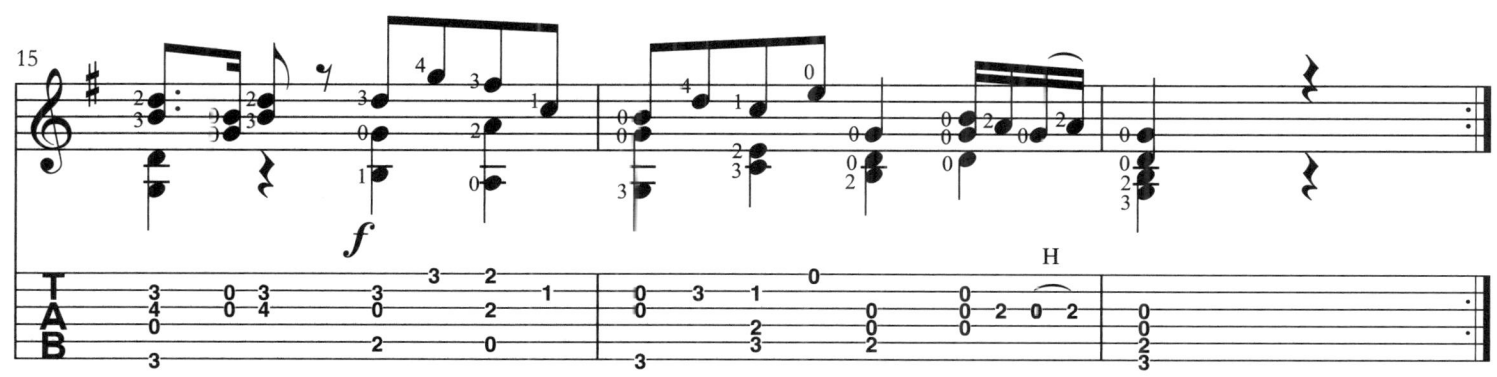

# DROP D AND G TUNING

Many pieces written for classical guitar, or arranged for classical guitar, require certain strings to be tuned differently than normal. We call these *alternate tunings*. The most common alternate tuning is called *Drop D* tuning, which calls for tuning the 6th string down one whole step, from E to D. For "Maple Leaf Rag," we first go into Drop D, and then also lower the 5th string one whole step from A to G to create *drop G* tuning.

The easiest way to get into an alternate tuning is with an electronic tuner—either a dedicated device or a downloaded app. For this particular tuning, it is easy to match the 6th string D to the open 4th string D an octave higher, and the 5th string G to the open 3rd string G, also an octave higher.

*Excerpt from*
## Maple Leaf Rag
 Track 86

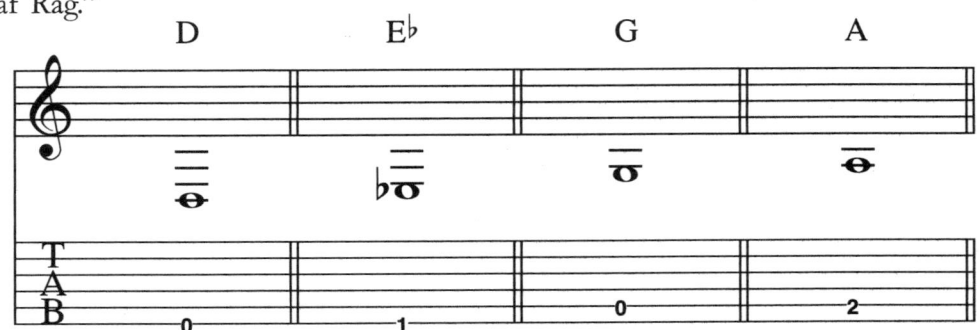

Here are the notes played on the 6th (low D) and 5th (low G) strings in "Maple Leaf Rag."

by Scott Joplin

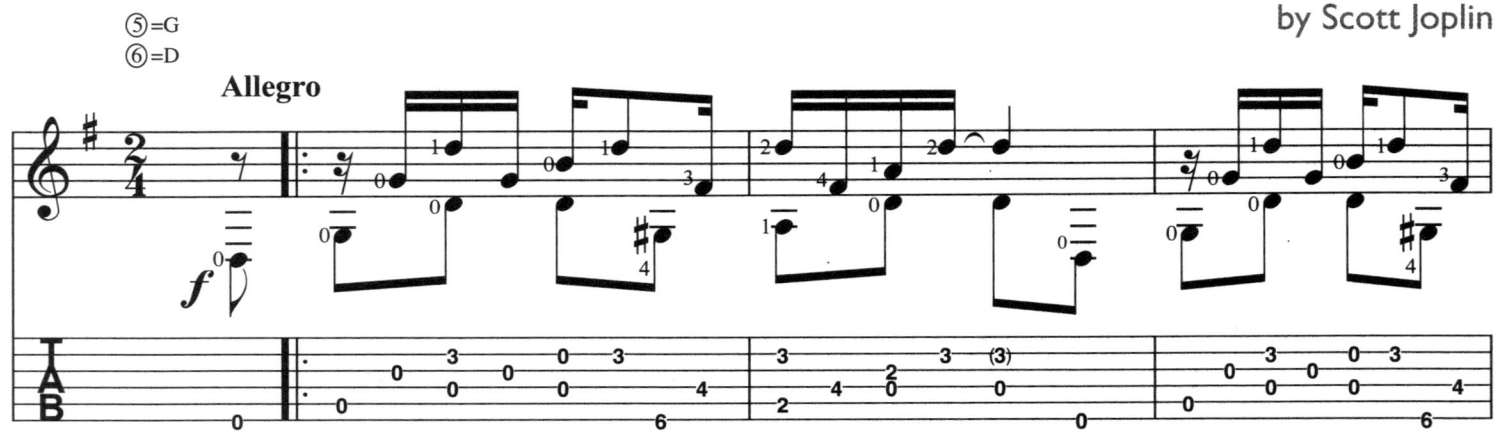

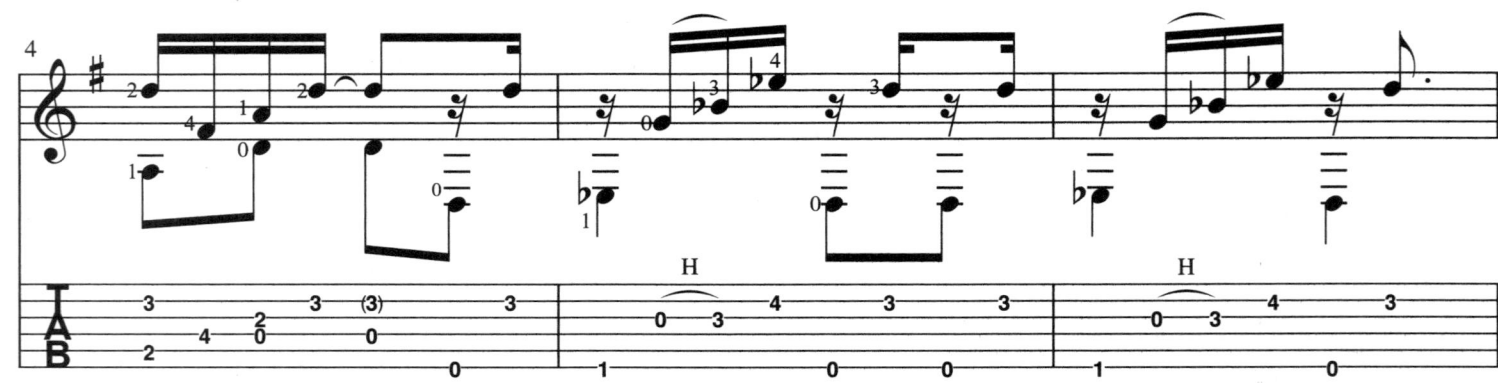

# TEACH YOURSELF TO PLAY CLASSICAL GUITAR

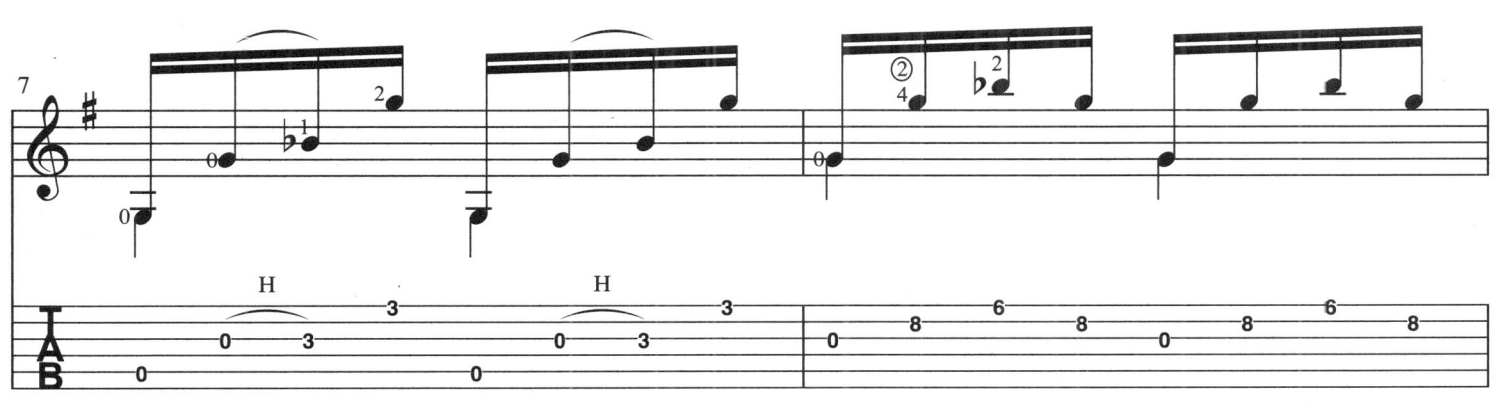

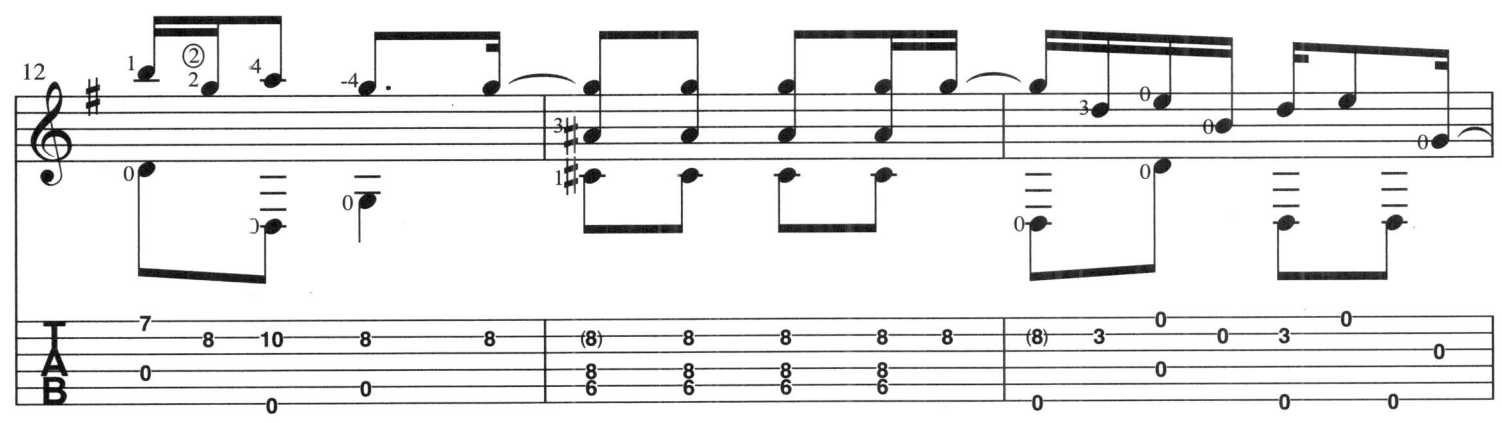

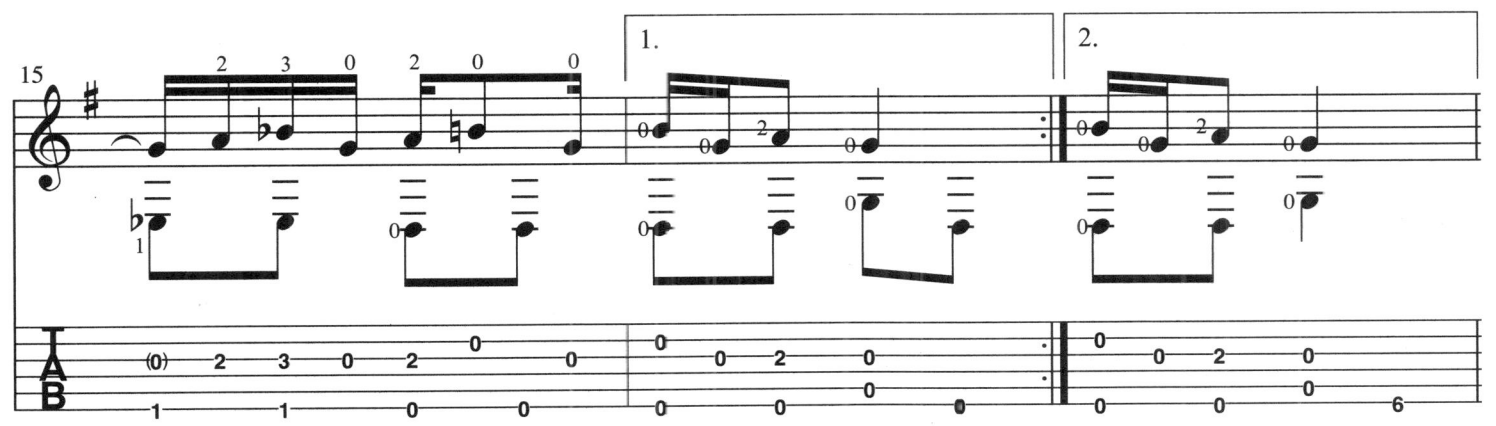

# Piano Concerto No. 3, Movement 1 (Theme)  Track 87

*Allegretto* is slightly slower than Allegro.

by Ludwig van Beethoven

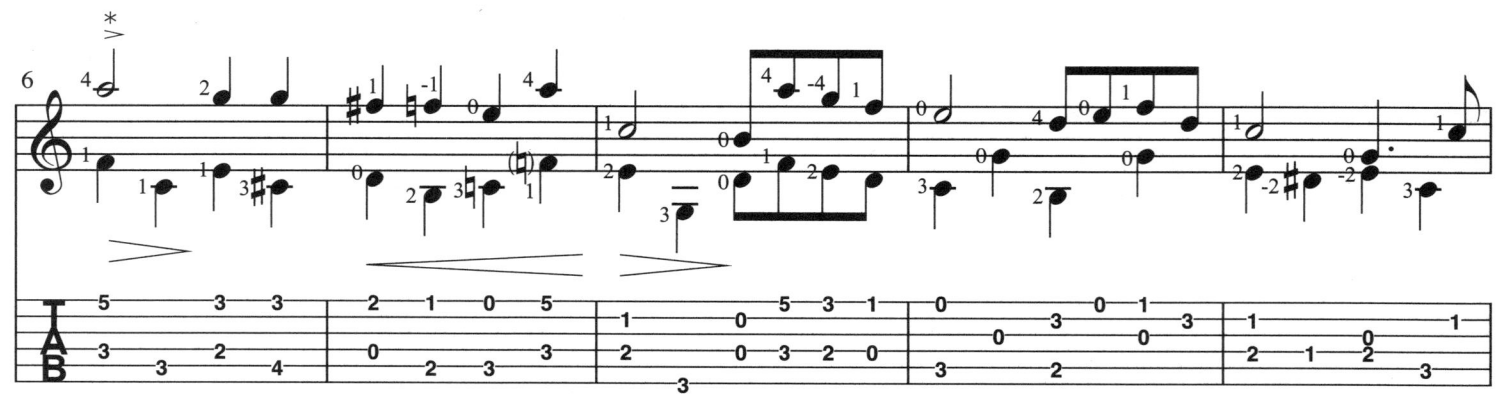

* This is an *accent*. Play this note a bit louder.

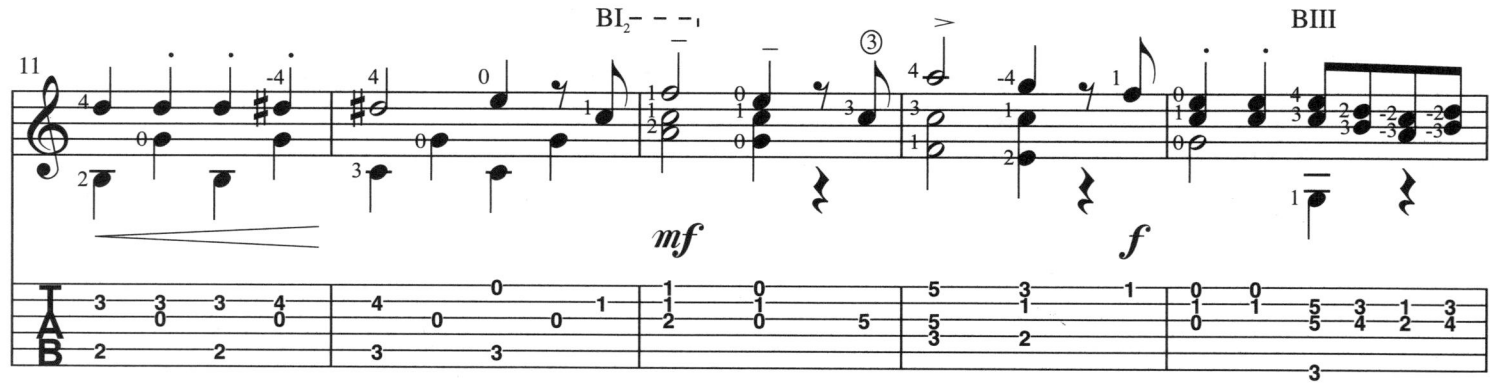

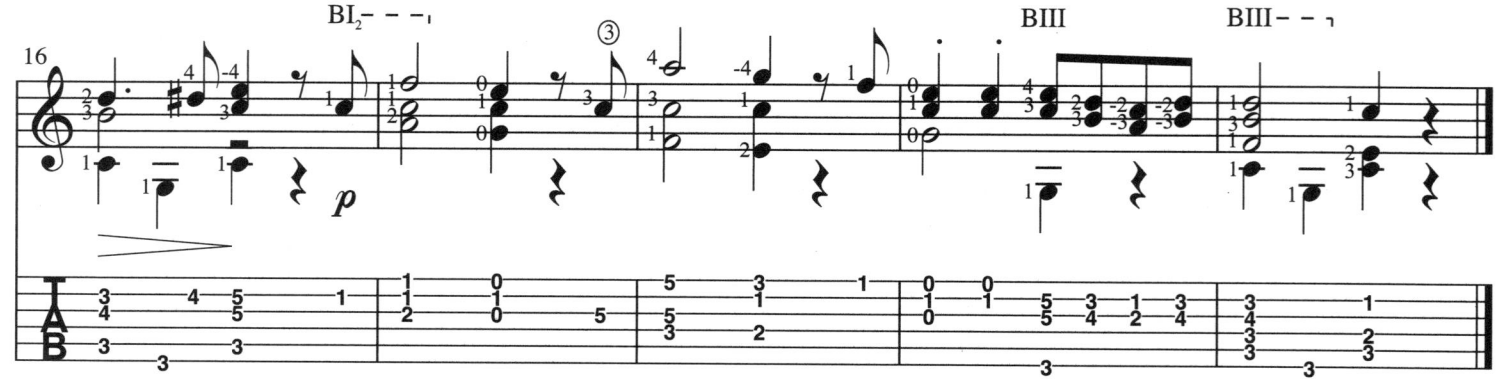

Congratulations! You're a classical guitarist! It's time to find a great teacher and keep on learning. You're just getting started and there's always more to learn. Take your time, and practice, practice!